Normal 2016

Selected Works from

The Third Annual

David Foster Wallace Conference

Normal 2016

Selected Works from
The Third Annual
David Foster Wallace Conference

Jeff Jarot, Ashlie Kontos,
Brian Monday, and Carissa Kampmeier, Eds.

Copyright © 2017 Lit Fest Press

All Work Property of Individual Authors and Artists

Cover Image: Copyright © 2017 Chris Ayers

All rights reserved

ISBN: 978-1-943170-24-1

Cover Art: Chris Ayers

Interior and Cover Design: Jane L. Carman

Published by Lit Fest Press, Carman, 688 Knox Road 900 North, Gilson, Illinois 61436

Outside the box

Table of Contents

Introduction
  Brian Monday — xi

Digital Marginalia
  Corrie Baldauf — 1

Some Thoughts on the Aesthetics of *Infinite Jest*
  Ben Leubner — 7

Infinite Jest as an Art Object
  Tom Winchester — 17

"Touch-Artist[s] and Thinker[s]": Moving Beyond the Phenomenological Subject in *Infinite Jest*
  G. M. Bettendorf — 21

The Bad Storks: Dad-diction in *The Dream Songs* and *Infinite Jest*
  Daniel Leonard — 33

The Darkly Delicious Thing: Explorations of the Gothic in *Infinite Jest*
  Melissa Holton — 43

Who's There: I am: Ghosts and Intertextuality in *Infinite Jest*
  Melissa Newfield — 53

Infinite Jest, Postmodernism, and Irony: A Brief Guide
to Happiness in Our Contemporary Age
   Alexander C. Ruhsenberger   65

David Foster Wallace, Heidegger, and Postmodern Irony
   Danny Sheaf   75

Is an Antidepressant a Ramp or a Prosthesis?
The Nonendogenous Literature of David Foster Wallace
   Rhett Farinholt   89

from *Zuzu's Petals*
   Jeff Jarot   97

"Spectral Apostrophe" and *The Inkiest Black*
   Barbara Balfour   105

from "Exit Interview"
   Jane L. Carman   111

from "Exit Interview"
   Amy L. Eggert   119

Author Biographies   123

Introduction

If the term *classic* is problematic, then its descendent, the *contemporary classic*, and its no-less-oxymoronic twin, the *modern classic*, must be bent double with complications, twisted with disorders due to centuries of literary inbreeding. One such monstrous child is David Foster Wallace's *Infinite Jest*, along with its many siblings that likewise vie for contemporary-classic standing.

In *Why Read the Classics*, Italo Calvino identifies 14 qualities or definitions of the classic, several of which seem applicable to the *contemporary classic* and to Wallace's work. Of all Calvino's definitions, the one most relevant here and to the anthology you hold is #8: "A classic is a work which constantly generates a pulviscular cloud of critical discourse around it, but which always shakes the particles off." What other writer of Wallace's generation is more pulviscularly productive? In this regard, Wallace is the Pig-Pen, the haboob, of contemporary authors: the reader who dares fall asleep with one of Wallace's books in his lap wakes to find himself buried to the nose in a dune of critical discourse.

But what else qualifies *Infinite Jest* or *The Pale King* or any other of Wallace's books as a contemporary classic? Perhaps the most direct answer lies at the level of the sentence. As William Gass argues in "To a Young Friend Charged with Possession of the Classics," superior sentences are what all classics share in common—not their truth or goodness, but the sentences that comprise them: "sentences that take such notice of the world that the world seems visible in their pages, palpable, too, so a reader might fear to touch those paragraphs concerned with conflagrations or disease or chicanery lest they be victimized, infected or burned." Consider the following sentence from *The Broom of the System*, in which sometimes-narrator Rick Vigorous reconstructs the scene of the Mount Holyoke Mixer of '68:

> In any event, there were we, grouped in blue suits and gray suits and slicked-back hair and shiny nervous noses, and there were they, a sweet shifting miasma of wool, shaped hair, cashmere, eyes, cotton, calves and pearls, in the midst of which she stood, by the hors d'oeuvre bar, in a skirt and monogrammed sweater, talking quietly with friends, conspicuously danceless all night, and it was close to twelve, and there were we, in suits, gathering our saliva for the final assault. (211)

The scene ends comitragically when Rick launches, to his horror, an "enormous glob of the chewed hors d'oeuvre, the Ritz cracker and bologna, chewed, with saliva in it, with shocking force…on the fleshy part of Janet Dibdin's nose.…" But first, consider the architecture of the sentence above, as Rick conveys the charged inevitability of the scene in the parallel clauses of "there were we" and "there were they" and again "and there were we." Rick's stilted grammar, also apparent in the stretch "in the midst of which she stood," divulges his meagre or at least overtaxed literary aptitude, but it is often blended with Wallace's own *un*stilted voice, such as in the liquid, polysyndeton'd syntax of this line: "grouped in blue suits and gray suits and slicked-back hair." Here, and throughout the novel, is an irresolvable interplay between Rick's style, as narrator, and Wallace's style, as author—the former producing the pretty awful Fieldbinder entries as well as some of the most beautiful passages of the novel. We also see here Wallace's penchant for the comically absurd ("shiny nervous noses" and "gathering our saliva for the final assault"); his atomic noticing of detail ("a sweet shifting miasma of wool, shaped hair, cashmere, eyes, cotton, calves and pearls"), detail that's cubistically rendered, as parts of the female dancers' fashion commingle with elements of their own bodies, suggestive of the excited, collective male ogling of the girls; his careful, often surprising word selection ("sweet…miasma," as if the sight of the girls is too much, paradoxically sickening, and then "assault," with its suggestion of potential violence that harks back to the novel's opening dorm-room scene); and his infusion of the pathetic ("conspicuously danceless all night, and it was close to twelve") with the bathetic ("gathering our saliva" and "it flew out and landed on the fleshy part of Janet Dibdin's nose, and stayed there"). So, yes, in this single sentence Wallace's world is visible and palpable: the reader fully feels Rick's mortification and cringes at it, remembering her own crushing moments of public humiliation just as sadly comedic to some bystanding audience, yet she laughs despite herself with Wallace at the absurdity of the scene (this time she's thankfully one of the bystanders!) and marvels at Wallace's perfect timing, selection of detail, and turns of phrase. The reader nearly fears that that "enormous glob" will fly off the page and onto the tip of her own nose.

The Illinois State University David Foster Wallace Conference is another testament to the contemporary-classic standing of Wallace's work—to the extent of scholarship, the range of critical approaches, the variety of readership, and the degree of veneration that Wallace's work continues to engender. This last conference—held in Stevenson Hall, a move that afforded attendees a new closeness to the environment in which Wallace worked and taught for nearly a decade—again affirmed Wallace's work's ability to generate a dust cloud of discourse only to "shake the particles off." The presentations covered well the body of Wallace's work, though *Infinite Jest* garnered the most attention and *The Broom of the System* perhaps the least, which is interesting to me. *Broom* is the Wallace text I know best, as I've taught it for the last two years to my high school AP students, and I would ask critics and scholars not to forget its place in the Wallace oeuvre. It is a work that contains nearly all the same rewards of Wallace's later work, despite the author's abashed dismissal of it ("that old thing…," perhaps only a pose), and a work that possesses a certain levity, ease, and unapologetic attitude toward its experimental exuberance perhaps absent from his later fiction. *Broom* serves as a harbinger of the key features and themes of Wallace's later writing, and transports its reader to the beginning of Wallace's career with all its reeling promise. My students overwhelmingly praise the book, at year's end, set alongside other 20th century classics: *The Metamorphosis* (also universally loved), *To the Lighthouse* (usually gains only one zealot in the class), and *Pnin* (draws a faction of loyalists).

Gender studies, disability studies, politics and postmodern irony, theology and literary journalism, phenomenology and psychoanalytic criticism, democracy and second-wave feminism, concerns of translation and film adaptation, of aesthetics and narrative structures—conference presenters applied all these approaches and more, yet when we return to our homes and to Wallace's work, all the discourse falls away, the dust cloud clears, leaving Wallace speaking to us in his inimitable voice and style. I think of Madame Psychosis and her intimate MIT-and-slightly-beyond audience—her mesmerizing voice drifting over the "florid-purple nighttime breath of the historic Charles river" (184), bringing succor to all who are lonely or lost: "Come one come all…."—the way Wallace reaches his readers who, Mario-like, "listen the way other kids watch TP, opting for mono and sitting right up close…staring into that special pocket of near-middle distance reserved for the serious listener." When reading his own work, Wallace, too, had a voice "sparely modulated and strangely empty, as if [he] were speaking from inside a small box…not bored or laconic or ironic….[rather] reflective but not judgmental…low-depth familiar…the way certain childhood smells will strike you as familiar and oddly sad" (189). And as with Madame Psychosis' program, "over time some kind of pattern emerges" in Wallace's books, "a trend or rhythm," and we're "somehow sure" Wallace cannot himself "sense the compelling beauty and light [he] projects over the air somehow…" (190).

Having attended the first three years of this conference, I've seen how it has not only provided a venue and audience for dozens and dozens of original papers but has also brought readers, critics, and scholars together. Attendees have made lasting connections, even friendships. They have heard and met writers of great stature, including D. T. Max, Stephen J. Burn, and last year, Marshall Boswell, and have met and heard personal accounts from those colleagues who knew Wallace best, colleagues such as Charles and Victoria Harris, Robert McLaughlin and Sally Parry. In returning to ISU, I feel something like Rick Vigorous with all his nostalgia when he visits his (and Wallace's) alma mater, Amherst College, though I left no initials scrawled on the bathroom stalls of The Cellar or The Gallery to search out years later. But I can only imagine what other attendees coming from all over the country, even the world, might feel in walking the same streets and halls and eating at the same restaurants as Wallace, as they perhaps tour the suggested places of DFW significance now outlined by The Bloomington-Normal Area Convention and Visitors Bureau, including Cracker Barrel, Babbitt's Books, and Wallace's home.

Now for an epithet for the Wallace devotee, for all those "serious listeners" of his who, like Great Gramma Lenore in her devotion to Wittgenstein, carry around a copy of *Infinite Jest*, though too large for any pocket. Something akin to the disciples of Nabokov (Nabokophile) or Austen (Janeite). DFWphile? Daveite? Fantod, howling with laughter and admiration?

Brian Monday
August 20, 2016

Digital Marginalia
Corrie Baldauf

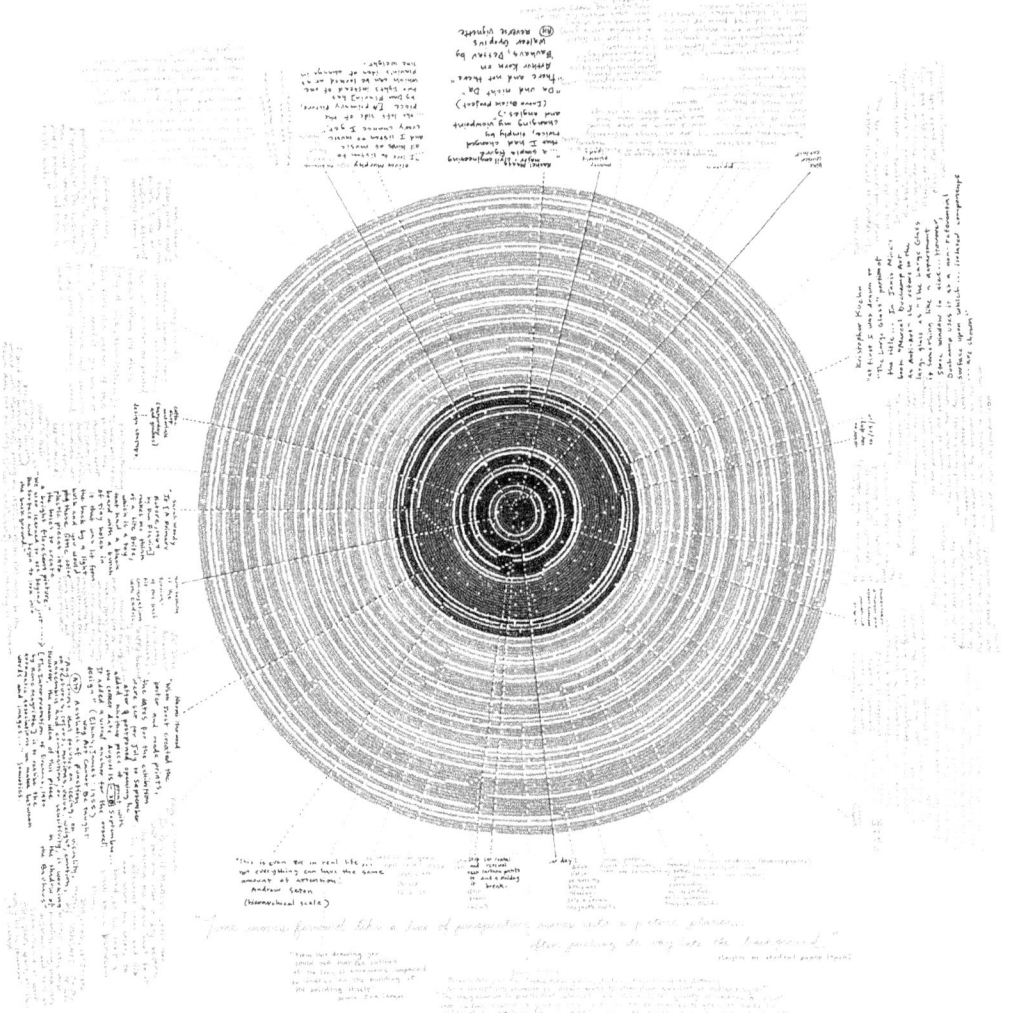

Corrie Baldauf
Time Moves Forward, 2012

What happens when marginalia reaches the edges of the page? Does it stop? Or does it start to tumble out into the world, out of your mouth and through your fingers onto keyboards and screens?

———

After David Foster Wallace, here is still here, but we are as well. Is it the Year of Xfinity? Or Clarity? It is still the Year of Xfinity. Consider that it is possible to relate this timing and chaos to new forms of efficiency and, eventually, clarity.

What happens when we look at the themes in Wallace's writing in relation to the people with whom we live and work? Is it possible to talk about Wallace without referencing his name? This is a game-like avenue to having conversations about what we are thinking about within Wallace's writing with people who otherwise may not be interested.

Some of the names and subject matter I reference will likely be new and may at first seem unrelated. This is intentional, and I hope that it pushes our thought processes in new directions. Afterwards, in mere minutes, it may still be possible to go right back to the way we were thinking before this conversation. Know that no matter how disparate any of the themes and the content seem, everything links back to the virtual conversations that have transpired between speakers and participants at the 2015 and 2016 David Foster Wallace conferences.

———

Ruth Koelewyn (artist) shared an article with me that questions our consistent reliance on synchronous systems. The action of repeating an author's name, throughout a series of conference or online conversations, is in itself synchronous. At first, it does create focus and order, but out of context, this type of repetition has the potential to exclude the people whom we hope to include.

Mike Pepi (writer) explains, "Synchrony…is comparable to a dictatorship, Rules, Fordism, assembly lines…all you can really do is speed it up." He also offers an alternative: "Asynchrony is needed to break through the barrier of scalable systems." In other words, is obvious order always faster?

"Synchronous and clocked" is comparable to assembly line models. If we were going to assembly-line a double-stacked tray of wine glasses from one side of this room to the other, we would be engaging in an orderly prescription in a way that might look like an old strand of series circuit lights, continuously handing glasses to the people closest to us unless one of us fell over. Then, unlike machine assembly lines, hopefully we would stop.

Expanding to an asynchronous system, with Mac or our lit procedure of getting the glasses moved, would first result in chaos. If we all rushed this double stack of wine glasses, we would all drop more. Likely, this could be prevented. In an asynchronous system, the only time any one of us would go all the way to the tray to get a glass would be when we were not occupied by a glass being passed from somewhere else in the room, closer to the other side or to our destination.

———

Where are you now? Where were you the week before the 2016 David Foster Wallace Conference?

———

There, where we each were earlier, and here, where we are raging. Only again and again, in fragments between and amidst work hours and screens, aligning with poet Billy Collins in *Marginalia*:

raging along the borders of every page
we pressed a thought into the wayside,
planted an impression along the verge. (3) (36-38)

In a similar space, Andrea Eis, Associate Professor of Film Studies at Oakland University, takes marginalia found in Greek texts to celebrate "the pleasure of words in the margins," through photography and film.

In 2008 Eis discovered Meta Glass (that really was her name) at the International Center for Hellenic and Mediterranean Studies in Athens, Greece. Her marginalia filled twenty Greek books.

Eis found a link to feed the process of photographing Glass' marginalia in the *New York Times Magazine*, where Sam Anderson describes how "…[marking up books is a way] to fully enter a text, to collaborate with it, to mingle with an author." Anderson describes marginalia as addictive. "Writing in them [books] is the closest I come to meditation; marginalia is— no exaggeration— possibly the most pleasurable thing I do on a daily basis."

Anderson points out an example of his marginalia in Chapter 4 of *Great Expectations*, featuring this hyperbole of a visual description:

"I remember Mr. Hubble as a tough high-shouldered stooping old man, of a sawdusty fragrance, with his legs extraordinarily wide apart: so that in my short days I always saw some miles of open country between them when I met him coming up the lane."

This excerpt gets me thinking about how possible it is to omit the defining boundaries of both marginalia and ekphrasis. Andrew Thompson (sculptor and professor) and I have spent several summer hours comparing what is occurring outside the margins of the pages we are reading to what is happening outside buildings that house art. Curator Pamela Hart describes ekphrasis as an "…exchange between artists and writers." Think further than Dorian Gray.

Look at the edges of pages and screens as fluidly as the edges of a book made out of ice. Artist Justin James Reed made a sculpture of ice that is the shape and size of a book. Consider how the translucent ice in your drink, next to your book or laptop, contributes to the texts we are reading.

What did you walk on to get to your reading spot? Could you feel the surface through your shoes? Artist Rachel Libeskind freezes the moment of turning and absorbing open pages in a book sculpture made of concrete.

Are the things under the benches at the train station comparable to the things described in the text? Where are you in relation to the time and place of the writing? Artist Moses Hoskins drags this stuff all the way into the binding of his book sculptures.

How about at diners?

On Thomas Pynchon finding meaning at diners… I laughed when I noticed bananas on my breakfast menu as I was putting it under my copy of *Gravity's Rainbow*. How does this real-time information expand the printed text?

Have you ever scrolled through an article and realized the flicks of your hand were congruous with the sounds of the song coming through the speakers?
———

Now, let's get back to our conference and the conversations surrounding it. In preparation for our 2016 David Foster Wallace Conference presentation, Mike Miley sent a note to Matthew Luter and me about a book called *The World Beyond Your Head*. What if the title itself is a method for describing digital marginalia?

Pull-quoting text and reacting to it on social media are forms of digital marginalia that have the potential to become a conversation. Think about the way a Post-It Note extends beyond the edge of a computer screen, pointing both to and away from the backlit text. Check out to whom or what a Post-It Note is pointing the next time you see one protruding from a monitor. Who is it? Does it make sense to have a conversation using Wallace's name, one of our names, or is it best to jump right into the subjects and themes that reach beyond synchronous systems?

You should always think about the other. And the trust. The listening has to be complete.
—Esther Shalev-Gerz

Art is the hammer with which we shape our reality.—Brecht

_____

Works Cited

Pepi, Mike.. "Asynchronous! On the Sublime Administration of the Everyday." *E-Flux* #74, June 2016, www.e-flux.com/journal/asynchronous-on-the-sublime-administration-of-the-everyday.
Collins, Billy. "Marginalia" *Poetry Foundation*.
Dickens, Charles. *Great Expectations*. London: Chapman & Hall, 1861.

Some Thoughts on the Aesthetics of *Infinite Jest*
Ben Leubner

Reflection upon feeling contents itself with the observation of the subjective affection in its isolation, instead of diving into and fathoming the matter in question itself, the work of art, and, while engaged with it, simply letting go the mere subjectivity and its states. In feeling it is just this vacant subjectivity that is not merely retained, but given the first place, and that is why men are so fond of having emotions. And for the same reason such a study becomes tedious from its indefiniteness and vacancy, and repulsive from its attentiveness to little subjective peculiarities. (38)—Hegel's *Introductory Lectures on Aesthetics*

I.
This is the kind of remark one would expect to find in an early 19th century treatise or lecture on aesthetics. It insists on the autonomy, integrity, even the objective quality of the work of art over and against the contingency of the subjective feelings of whoever encounters it. Implied in the remark is a standard of taste, of aesthetic appreciation, to be aimed for, one that discounts feelings, where to focus on and cultivate one's own feelings in response to art is therefore *not* to develop the faculty of taste. We are given two options when confronted with a work of art: to focus on the work of art itself at the expense of our "little subjective peculiarities," or to focus on what we feel at the expense of the work. Hegel recommends the former and denigrates the latter, which is to say that he gives precedent to the work of art, locating in it the source of beauty and in the process relegating the self to a secondary position. Despite its having been created by a human being, the human being takes a back seat to the work of art and is of secondary importance when considered in light of its existence. The creation trumps the creator, and beauty is certainly not in the eye of the beholder but is instead very much in the beheld.

These implications and others embedded in Hegel's remark underwent numerous variations over subsequent decades, but the general gist of the remark held sway at least through the mid-20th century and the reign of the

New Criticism, at the core of which were similar notions concerning the autonomy of art. Once the theory boom started, however, the assumptions latent in this kind of approach to aesthetics came under heavy attack—aesthetics *itself* came under heavy attack, in fact, with, certainly, a number of positive results, not the least of which was a dismantling of the hegemony of a Eurocentric philosophy of art that had insisted on its universal application under the pretense of its being a science.

There were also negative results of this dismantling of Western aesthetics, though, including, perhaps, a massive spike in *ego*-centrism as a consequence of the enthroning of the very feelings in matters of taste, too much emphasis upon which Hegel cautions us will result in tedium, indefiniteness, and vacancy. To displace the work of art from the center of the aesthetic experience in favor of putting oneself there, that is, results in the creation of a new problematic, a problematic the implications of which we see painstakingly drawn out in the work of Wallace, much of whose work is preoccupied with the question of how to *de*center the self in favor of something made greater than it precisely by virtue of its being placed at the center of the self's experience. The alleviation of loneliness cannot be brought about by finding the right thing to satiate the ego, whether it be another person, an illicit substance, fame, or one of countless other forms of entertainment and distraction. Such a desire for satiation continues to work with a world picture that presumes that the self is always at the center of its own experience and so vacuums other things towards itself, engendering the very thing it seeks to mitigate in the process: its own isolation. These are the fruits of a predominantly American, consumer-oriented aesthetic, one that insists not on the autonomy of the work of art and a resultant diminishment of the person encountering it but instead on the consumer's inalienable right to be sated, soothed, pleased, and entertained by an art that, far from making strenuous demands, caters and administers to him. It is this very world picture that stands in need of revision if endemic loneliness is to be addressed in an effective manner. It is less a question of *what* the self needs to bring to itself in order to cure its affliction than of *how* the self can remove itself from the center of its own experience, the source *of* its affliction. Here a return to the aesthetics of the late 18th and early 19th century might prove of considerable use, where the troublesome aspects of those aesthetics need not prevent us from seizing upon their virtues.

The either/or choice between the work of art and our own subjective peculiarities implied in the remark from Hegel with which I began, upon close examination, and especially when considered in light of how the next two centuries unfolded when it came to aesthetics, quickly ceases to be at all simple but instead splits up and produces a mesh of considerations, the untangling of which presents immense difficulties, just as the Eschaton debacle finds Hal "riveted at something …that seems so terribly abstract and fraught with implications and consequences that even thinking about how to articulate it seems so completely stressful that being almost incapacitated with absorption is almost the only way out of the complex stress" (340). As a result, the dilemma proposed by Hegel was one that baffled and intrigued Wallace throughout his career, entailing as it did an historical sequence that concerned him gravely and of which he has since become an important part. One can see Wallace grappling with the choice proposed in Hegel's remark in every genre to which he applied himself: from short stories, novels, and nonfiction to sports writing, interviews, and commencement addresses. Furthermore, one could certainly do worse than to say that this dilemma in the history of aesthetics, along with all its attendant ramifications, lies at the very heart of *Infinite Jest*, in its concern with addiction, entertainment, and ruin; repetition, diminishment, and perfection; with what we *choose*: the self or something made greater than it precisely by virtue of being granted primacy over it.

The general tendency today is to denigrate Hegelian aesthetics and all its variations in favor of the attitude that posits that art is essentially what one makes of it and that art appreciation is therefore entirely subjective. Nevertheless, consider, just for the sake of a thought experiment, what happens when the remark from Hegel's lectures is applied not to our encounters with art but rather to our encounters with other people. Our options remain the same: on the one hand, we can conduct ourselves in relation to others with our own feelings first and foremost in our minds; on the other hand, we can we can dive into the matter of that which we are encountering with the aim of understanding it on its own terms, putting our own feelings aside in favor of showing consideration to something external to ourselves. Hegel favors the latter option, but it is precisely this option and its virtues that are touted in arguments often made *against* the essentialisms of much of western philosophy, including Hegel. That is, Hegel's preference for a non-subjective, anti-egoistic approach to aesthetics is attacked for being massively egoistic and subjective. Even our attacks on Hegel, it would seem, are Hegelian. However that may be, though, and despite the clear force with which the second of the two options just delineated recommends itself as the more ethical approach to our encounters with others, it seems quite clearly to be the case that American culture and society are predicated upon the first. We have used Hegel's own logic against him in order to be rid of him, that we might therefore adopt a method of existing in relation to both art and to each other, a method that his logic expressly forbids. We want to insist on the primacy of our own minute, subjective peculiarities while at the same time devising an argument that makes this an ethically viable position.

We would perhaps be better off were we to heed Hegel here wittingly and directly, rather than renouncing him via his own logic in favor of what he himself refers to as the tedious, indefinite, vague, and repulsive insistence we place on tending to our own feelings and emotions above all other things, whether it be a work of art or another person. Wallace certainly thought so anyway and says as much throughout *Infinite Jest*, particularly by way of the characters Schtitt and Marathe, neither of whom, of course, are American, and both of whom advocate the choice of something other than the self as something around which to build one's life. That is, Schtitt's convictions concerning tennis, that training in tennis, for example, is really "just training for citizenship," instruction in "learning to sacrifice the hot narrow imperatives of the Self—the needs, the desires, the fears, the multiform cravings of the individual appetitive will—to the larger imperatives of a team," but that such training seems almost futile in a country like the experialist, self-serving, pleasure-oriented United States—these convictions are identical to the convictions that Marathe relays to Steeply over the course of their conversation above Tucson, where Schtitt's having fallen in love with a tree as a teenager then becomes the counterpart to Marathe's love for his skullless wife, both cases serving to illustrate a kind of self-displacement that seems increasingly less likely, less possible, in a culture that prioritizes the "flat and short-sighted idea of personal happiness" over "privation and hardship and the discipline which hardship teaches" (82-3). Thus the German-speaking Schtitt and the French-speaking Marathe critique American consumer culture, where the pursuit of happiness has metamorphosed from an already distinctly American inalienable right (Locke's original trio being life, liberty, and property) into an endless sequence of pleasure quests predicated upon media-generated images of beauty that perversely equate beauty with flawlessness. The pursuit of happiness itself, that is, has been reduced to the pursuit of a brand of pleasure, the need for which regenerates itself without fail, where both works of art and other people now become useful only insofar as they provide each isolated subject with a pleasurable, reassuring feeling, and where it is ultimately even less a case of any actual pursuit of pleasure than a clamoring for its *delivery*, for our right *to be pleased*. Life, liberty, and the delivery of pleasure through multiple channels—one of Wallace's aims in *Infinite Jest* is to illustrate the insidious manner by way of which the third, far from guaranteeing, engendering, or enhancing the first two, first curtails and then eliminates them.

II.
Infinite Jest is, like Johnny Gentle's Clean U. S. Party's project for "American renewal," an "essentially aesthetic affair" (383). However, whereas Gentle's main criteria for an ideal aesthetic effect are sterility, blemishlessness, and

immediate on-the-surface appeal, to the point where everything that does not meet these criteria is simply removed to a margin where it is hoped it can be safely ignored if not eliminated, Wallace's own criteria seem markedly different, his novel replete with infection, blemish, and instances of surface-level repulsion, and committed to the exposure of various hideous and improbable deformities that lurk within American culture. Nevertheless, it is no less an aesthetic affair.

The novel, of course, shares its title with the film that lies at the center of its plot, a film that would seem to function according to aesthetic principles antithetic to those of the novel and therefore more amenable to those of Gentle's party. Where the film is short, perfect in its surfaces (however wobbly), and utterly soothing, inducing in its watchers an ultimate passivity and disregard for anything outside the pleasure it induces, the novel is long and ungainly, frequently frustrating, and requires of its readers a diligent, active approach. Film and novel are thus opposites. The fact of the latter's containment of the former, however, in addition to their possessing the same name, gives the lie to this too-easy comparison, whereby the cumbersome, edifying book serves as an antidote to the sleek, entertaining film. For in a pertinent sense, one can claim that *Infinite Jest*, the novel, is itself sterile in its grammatical perfectionism, blemishless despite its own obsession with blemish, and it is nothing if not a novel of complete and total surface appeal. Furthermore, it is also, like the film it contains, immensely addictive, soothing, and gratifying, to the point that as soon as one finishes it, it is difficult to resist the temptation to immediately start it again, a temptation that the novel itself orchestrates. If the film, according to Molly Notkin, is purportedly some kind of "angelic monster of audience-gratification," then the novel that contains it is very much akin to it. It is, indeed, an angelic monster of reader-gratification, at least in the experience of this reader (791). No doubt the effect that *M*A*S*H* has on Steeply's father is meant to be seen as analogous to the effect that *Infinite Jest*, the film, has on its viewers, but it is also clearly anticipatory of the effect that *Infinite Jest*, the novel, will have on its readers: the production of near-total obsession; of notebooks filled with bizarre theories that explain or deduce what happens in the end; of color-coded marginalia and sticky notes; of conferences during which people congregate to advance all-important hypotheses concerning the book's meaning, and so on. Plenty of us read *Infinite Jest* in a state of near-obsession, occasionally pausing and "scribbling feverishly in [a] notebook," jotting down our "huge and complex theories about wide-ranging and deeply hidden themes having to do with death and time" within its pages (642, 644).

Infinite Jest, then, is neither novel-as-antidote to film and TV, nor is it novel-as-film or TV; it is somehow both, caught up no less in a concern for "American renewal" than Gentle's C.U.S.P. even as it mocks that party. It is a novel, the diving into and fathoming of which affords us the opportunity to decenter ourselves in relation to our own experience. Moreover, it is a novel that caters to our need to be pleased and entertained, and so it confirms our notion of ourselves as occupying a kind of central position of privilege around which everything else, the novel included, revolves, which it must serve. It is the one masquerading as the other—but which is which? It is what Wallace wanted it to be: as devastatingly pretty as the character within it, who stars in the film that provides it with its title—a character who is also hideously deformed.

Infinite Jest is also a repetitive novel about repetition in any number of forms, from the repetition of various tennis strokes in the pursuit of perfection to the repetition of the ingestion of substances in the pursuit of oblivion. What is especially of note here is the vital function that repetition plays in aesthetic experience, where one might even say that it is the key thereto. It is not just that we want to read a novel again, watch the film once more, listen to the song over and over; it is that we need to, in order to develop a full appreciation for the work of art in question. Full aesthetic appreciation requires this of us; it demands a familiarity born of repeated encounters. Nevertheless, at a certain point, something interesting happens, and the effect is reversed: too much repetition results in a lessening of the quality of the aesthetic experience. Eventually, you have read the book too many times, seen the film too often, listened to the song to death. There is a point in the process of repetition at which the returns cease to increase, cease, even, to remain on their highest plateau, and instead begin to diminish. In sum, the drug ceases to work.

A kind of ideal aesthetic effect, then, would perhaps be one that *never diminished*, regardless of the amount of repetition in which one indulged. A song that never became old, a drug, the effect of which never lessened, or, of course, a film—or book—one could watch—or read—again and again with no consequent diminishment of pleasure. Such an experience is, in an important sense, what many of the characters in the novel either have been or are seeking, whether it is via drugs or tennis, television or sex, or the practice of capturing animals in trash bags and killing them. However, as ideal as such a chased-after experience would in a certain regard be if actually attained, it seems that diminishment is, in reality, built into the nature of how we perceive beauty, that the effect must of necessity, at a certain point in the chain of repetitions, begin to wear off, where one might even aver that the true total aesthetic experience, however paradoxically, is only completed at the point at which the perception of beauty and the diminishment of its effect converge. There is something elegant and sad in this that Orsino formulates in the opening speech of *Twelfth Night*, during which first, having heard a lovely strain of music, he demands, "Give me excess of it that, surfeiting, / The appetite may sicken and so die," and then, accordingly, protests shortly thereafter, "Enough; no more; / 'Tis not so sweet now as it was before." (I, I, 7-8). He then says of the human capacity for the love of beauty that

> nought enters there,
> Of what validity and pitch soever,
> But falls into abatement and low price
> Even in a minute! (I, i, 11-14)

The source of the lethality of *Infinite Jest*, the film, is therefore that it never elicits the Duke's protest, "Enough!" and subsequent ruminations on the abatement of aesthetic pleasure but rather pleases so thoroughly and without diminishment as to leave its viewer caught in a state in which excess and surfeit is not possible. It is thus that the A.F.R. needs to be certain "that there could be no index of diminishing satisfaction as in the econometrics of normal U.S.A. commodities" when it comes to *Infinite Jest* (727), where in this regard these specific econometrics (of "normal U.S.A. commodities") are coextensive with those of the larger sphere of aesthetic experience itself, insofar as there is normally always at least some kind of index of diminishing satisfaction.

Thus, if the effect which art produces in us must necessarily wane, at least from time to time, then *Infinite Jest*, the film, is perhaps less a work of art than it is a work of pure and total entertainment, insofar as its effect never fades, wears off, diminishes, or perishes (where the late 15th century original meaning of "to entertain" was "to keep someone in a certain frame of mind"). The film is therefore not only some kind of ultimate aesthetic experience but rather is also, and perhaps is closer to, the antithesis thereof, as anesthetic as it is aesthetic, wherein what diminishes is not the effect of the experience but rather is the actual physical constitution of the person having it, for whom the source of pleasure also becomes the source of numbness and, eventually, death, as is the case with Narcissus, who never tires of staring at his own reflection, to the point that he slowly wastes away to nothing. Because his delight does not diminish, he of necessity must. It is a reversal of the more usual kind of aesthetic experience, whereby we eventually tire of the perceived beauty of the thing and so are not wholly consumed by it.

What is frightening, however, is that the ghost of such an effect as *Infinite Jest*, or Narcissus' own reflection, produces does in fact lurk within the "econometrics" of general aesthetic experience, whether it be those of "normal U.S.A. commodities" or, say, Shakespeare. For Steeply's father, for instance, *M*A*S*H* might as well be *Infinite Jest*—it certainly comes very close. Our attachments to, fetishes for, and obsessions with not only various shows, games, gifs, social media platforms, and so on, but also the technology by way of which we access them (where the former often seem to be but excuses or occasions for our addiction to the latter)—these attachments can indeed be severely debilitating, even to the point of becoming fatal. Death by *World of Warcraft* is a real thing. *Infinite Jest* is therefore now, in 2016, less a work of dystopian fiction than it is a clear illustration of the logical consequences of our society's grounding in and dependence on a technology of entertainment, a being held fast, that is to say, paralyzed, enthralled, by—and of—our own devices. Moreover, as Wallace knew, both the technology and the entertainment are only going to continue to become better. We are no doubt narcissistic now when it comes to our penchant for self-adulation, but it is possible that we are also quickly becoming narcissistic insofar as that penchant could turn out to be fatal. That is, there is less of a difference between Narcissus above the pool and an American before the screen than we would like to think; it is not just a cute comparison that ought to elicit a knowing smirk. After all, what we see when we stare at a television, computer, or smartphone screen is indeed an idealized reflection of ourselves staring back at us, a captivating super-image that subtends the crowd of actual images that greet our eyes, transfixing us just like the boy who looks into the pool and is captivated by his reflection. Furthermore, self-awareness in this regard is of little assistance; knowledge of what is happening is no guarantee of being able to free oneself from its effects. Narcissus, in Ovid's *Metamorphoses*, is under no illusion as to the occasion of his love; he knows it is his own reflection, an unsubstantial image, for which he pines, and yet he continues to yearn to grasp it. One could do worse than to posit that millennial American culture is a culture predicated upon love of and obsession with images that cannot be grasped, where the etymological meaning of "image" entails everything from phantoms and ghosts to reflections in mirrors.

Of course, it is all very well, and rather trendy, too, to posit that every time we engage in the aesthetic experience of watching television, going online, or opening an app, we subject ourselves to a form of paralysis from which it can sometimes be quite difficult to free ourselves. Thus, we lament the effects of current technologies and perhaps yearn for a time before their advent when we were not so easily seduced by the image. We should, perhaps, spend more time reading and less time on social media. The argument, indeed, is simplistic, as Wallace knew. A play is potentially no less enthralling, captivating, and paralyzing, capable of producing a stupor from which it indeed might be difficult to recover, than a sitcom. A book is no less a piece of technology dealing in images than a smartphone. The argument for why reading *Infinite Jest* is better for you than watching the film *Infinite Jest* cannot be made along the line of reasoning that simply posits that reading is better for you than viewing, for it is by no means clear that this is always necessarily the case. Wallace, certainly, wanted to interrogate this distinction, else he would not have given novel and film the same name. Nevertheless, am I then no less Narcissus when I open *Infinite Jest* than I am when I turn it on? Does the aesthetic effect of reading the novel also contain the ghost of the possibility of its producing the effect that the film it contains does? What should it be that makes reading so much better for us than viewing, to the point of positing the one as the key to education and enlightenment, and the other as the antithesis thereto, as we often do? Furthermore, what, then, of the ways in which the Internet so completely blurs the distinction between the two, between reading and viewing, making recourse to simple arguments about activity and passivity untenable?. In addition, wouldn't reading, then, anyway, be more passive than social media management, considerably so, at least from a certain point of view? Making the claim that reading is more *intellectually* engaging here is only somewhat satisfying. Here the idea is that reading *Infinite Jest* stimulates the mind and requires that it *work*, while watching the film *Infinite Jest* deadens it and results in its total passivity. There is definitely something to be taken from this, but it is not entirely as clear as all that. The two activities might be conceived as occupying opposite ends of a spectrum, but if you bend the line of the spectrum in such a way as to make it a circle, the two points meet and become one, where one would like to say that for Wallace, *this* was what really captivated, enthralled, and endlessly intrigued him, the fact that it can be so strangely difficult to tell the difference between the alleviation of loneliness through stimulating activity and its engendering through passive reception of stimuli.

In *The World as Will and Representation*, Arthur Schopenhauer, speaking of aesthetic contemplation, muses, "There always lies so near to us a realm in which we have escaped entirely from all our affliction; but who has the strength to remain in it for long" (198)? Here, he has in mind, despite his dislike of Hegel, something akin to Hegel's "diving into and fathoming the matter in question itself, the work of art, and, while engaged with it, simply letting go the mere subjectivity and its states." It is by virtue of letting go the mere subjectivity and its states that one escapes entirely from one's affliction, where what makes this possible is the aesthetic contemplation of nature or art. That is, Schopenhauer's position, like Hegel's, favors a view of aesthetic contemplation that, far from prioritizing "the mere subjectivity and its states," seeks to annul them by transcending them in favor of a focus upon that which is much less tedious and far more interesting: in this case, the work of art. However, to remain at such a pitch of concentration is not easy; it is easier by far, according to Hegel, to give first place to one's own "vacant subjectivity." Who indeed has the strength to remain in a state of fixed contemplation of something other than one's own self for very long?

Nevertheless, the most interesting thing, of course, about the quotation from Schopenhauer is how easily it can be said to describe not the act of reading *Infinite Jest* but rather the act of watching it. When I take up the novel, I do indeed find myself in a realm in which I am temporarily free from affliction insofar as I am removed from myself simply by virtue of the act of reading. Reading, Wallace felt, was one of the best cures for, or at least a form of alleviation of, loneliness. However, what is the gist of Marathe's proposal to Kate Gompert if not that there does indeed lie nearby a realm in which she can escape entirely from all her affliction, and that this realm is the one in which the viewer of *Infinite Jest* finds oneself? Only in this case, of course, it does not require great strength to remain in this realm for long but rather the opposite: it requires more strength than any human has to leave it. In both instances we are dealing with a form of escapism. In the case of reading the novel, though, what we escape from are the little subjective peculiarities of our own will, peculiarities, however, that have a strong magnetic pull on us and so make it difficult to sustain our removal from their midst for long periods of time, whereas in the case of watching the film, these peculiarities are soothed and lulled to the point of complete satiation, to the point where the ego is so massaged and affirmed that escape from its field is no longer either desirable or feasible. Again, what I think Wallace found particularly fascinating was just how difficult it can often be to distinguish these two states from one another, despite their seeming to be antithetical.

Works Cited

Hegel, George Wilhelm Friedrich. *Introductory Lectures on Aesthetics*. Trans. Bernard Bosanquet. Penguin Classics, 2004.
Schopenhauer, Arthur. *The World as Will and Representation, Vol. 1*. Trans. E. F. J. Payne. Dover, 1966.
Shakespeare, William. *Twelfth Night*. Ed. Barbara A. Mowat and Paul Werstine. Simon and Schuster: 2004.
Wallace, David Foster. *Infinite Jest*. Little, Brown, and Comoany, 1996.

Infinite Jest as an Art Object
Tom Winchester

Intermittent references to Gian Lorenzo Bernini's baroque-era artwork "The Ecstasy of Saint Teresa" serve to portray David Foster Wallace's *Infinite Jest* as an art object. The artwork provides context for the novel's ability to activate the reader as a character in its narrative in a style more akin to theater than literature. Writings by Arnold Hauser, Peter Bürger, and Michael Fried create the lens through which the novel's theatrical style can be seen.

"The Ecstasy of Saint Teresa" is a life-sized artwork sculpted from marble with gold detailing. It's presented in the Church of Santa Maria della Vittoria in Rome, Italy, where it towers over and envelops its viewers. The artwork depicts a theater with audience members watching the scene of a hovering angel jabbing a spear downward toward a climaxing St. Teresa. [fig. 1] Viewers of the artwork become witnesses not only to the events on stage, but also to the audience members who are depicted as watching the stage. The result is an acknowledgment of the viewers' world, which activates aspects outside of the artwork, including the viewer's environment and the act of viewing.

Arnold Hauser mentions such theatricality characteristic of the baroque era in his 1951 book, *The Social History of Art: Renaissance, Mannerism, Baroque*. "'[T]he tendency is to make a picture seem not a self-contained piece of reality, but a passing show in which the beholder has the good luck to participate just for a moment…'"[1] Such a description of the theatrical aspect of baroque art, and how it forced the participation of its viewers explains how "The Ecstasy of St. Teresa" can be seen as an icon for the style portrayed by *Infinite Jest*.

Either statement could be true of the novel's style: it's huge because its narrative is so long, or the reason its narrative is so long is because it needs to be huge. Both interpretations are possible when considering the idea that literature is the only medium which can effectively combat postmodernism's illusions because it still takes a long time to both produce and consume. Peter Bürger outlined this idea in his 1974 book, *Theory of the Avant-Garde*.

"[O]ne may summarize the importance of technical development has for the evolution of fine arts in these terms: because the advent of photography makes possible the precise mechanical reproduction of reality, the mimetic function of fine art withers. But the limits of this explanatory model become clear when one calls to mind that it cannot be transferred to literature. For in literature, there is no technical innovation that could have produced an effect comparable to that of photography in the fine arts."[2] With this statement it's possible to consider Wallace an artist working in the only medium capable of combatting a world reproduced to the point of simulation. What's beneficial about such a consideration is that it names a stylistic motivation not only behind the novel's gigantic size, but also, when combined with the idea of theatricality, sheds light on how *Infinite Jest* can be considered an art object.

Like an artist's book, the novel refers to it's own objecthood at certain points in the narrative, and such self-reference activates the reader as a player in the theater of reality. This is accomplished most effectively with the three-page correspondence between Helen Steeply and Marlon Bain, the presentation of which refers to the aspects of illusion in the reader's experience. The correspondence serves the narrative, but it's the presentation of the text on the page which is striking about this section. This is because nowhere else in the novel does a presentation of the text appear in a way that brings such tactile attention to both the objecthood of the paper and the actual act of reading. The tactile relationship the reader experiences is similar to the action of referring to the endnotes, or having to lug the dictionary-sized object, but is unique in that the text constructing the narrative self-referentially correlates with its presentation. In essence, the pages presented to the characters in the narrative become the actual pages the reader is holding in his or her hands, and, as a result, the reader is activated as an unwritten character in *Infinite Jest*.

In his 1967 essay, "Art and Objecthood," Michael Fried defines objecthood as the condition of non-art, and describes how art that doesn't seem like art, what he calls, "literalist art," activates those whose experience it in a theatrical way. "[E]spousal of objecthood amounts to nothing other than a plea for a new genre of theatre…Literalist sensibility is theatrical because, to begin with, it is concerned with the actual circumstances in which the beholder encounters a literalist work. Whereas in previous art 'what is to be had from the work is located strictly within [it],' the experience of literalist art is of an object in a situation – one that, virtually by definition, *includes the beholder…*"[3] Fried's idea of literalist art and how experiencing it activates its beholder's surroundings describes perfectly how these three pages activate readers in *Infinite Jest*. This is because the novel references itself most explicitly in this section, and therefore acknowledges aspects outside its text, including the reader and his or her surroundings.

Considering *Infinite Jest* as an art object helps to clarify why the novel looks and feels the way it does. Exemplary of a style more characteristic of the fine arts, the novel's theme of theatricality is signified by sporadic references to "The Ecstasy of Saint Teresa." Its objecthood combats the pitfalls of postmodernism by welcoming readers in to Wallace's world

Notes

[1] Arnold Hauser, *The Social History of Art Vol. 2: Renaissance, Mannerism, Baroque* (New York: Vintage Books, 1985), 177.
[2] Peter Bürger, *Theory of the Avant-Garde* (Minneapolis: University of Minnesota Press, 1984), 32.
[3] Michael Fried, "Art and Objecthood" (1967), Section III.

Figure

Tom Winchester, "The Ecstasy of St. Teresa" (2016)

"Touch-Artist[s] and Thinker[s]": Moving Beyond the Phenomenological Subject in *Infinite Jest*

G. M. Bettendorf

James O. Incandenza's final filmic effort, the *Infinite Jest* he created in the last 90 days of his life, was the product of the father-filmmaker's effort "to concoct something the gifted boy [Hal] couldn't simply master and move on from to a new plateau," as "a way to say I AM SO VERY, VERY SORRY and have it *heard*" (838-39, emphasis in original and text *sic*). The film, then, has a pretty clear apologetic tone. I will make use of the dual sense of the term "apology," arguing that it functions not only as an expression of paternal regret—Jim was never able to speak to or with Hal in any significant way—but also as a defense of *attempted* communication.

The first section of this paper treats Wallace's figuration of tennis as a primarily mental activity: in *Infinite Jest*, he is adamant that "real tennis" is a "hybrid" of "chess [and] boxing" (81), and elsewhere Wallace maintains that tennis "is chess on the run" ("Tornado Alley" 7). But, as I will suggest later, the sport's real significance to Wallace's work lies in what it reveals about the self's relationship to its body. Uncovering Wallace's treatment of limitations and boundaries through Maurice Merleau-Ponty's phenomenological lens helps us to expose the central thesis of *Infinite Jest*, which is that even though others can never truly know us (and, indeed, that we can never truly know our whole selves either), we can at least suggest to them that we have our own unique experiences of the shared world. Although language seems always to fail us, the very use of language, inadequate though it may be, signals to others that we exist, that we have consciousnesses, that we have rich interior lives—that we, like Hal, "have … intricate histor[ies]" and are infinitely "complex" (11).

1. "You're A Body, Jim": Curriculum and Pedagogy at Enfield Tennis Academy

At least in part, Wallace draws his approach towards tennis from personal experience, as his own childhood was not without athletic promise. His autobiographical essay "Derivative Sport in Tornado Alley" claims to treat his "near-great junior tennis" career (3) but really reads as a touching tribute to his homeland, the Midwest. Though Wallace here—famously—claims that "Midwest junior tennis was also [his] initiation into true adult sadness" (12), the essay also confirms Wallace's conception of tennis as an embodied activity, one that is necessarily mediated by the body's apparent situation in time and space.

In this essay, Wallace details what he terms an elusive "fugue-state that exhaustion through repetition brings on." In the "endless rally" of their drills, Wallace entered this "mental state at once flat and lush, numbing and yet exquisitely felt" (19):

> If both guys are good enough so that there are few unforced errors …, a kind of fugue-state opens up inside you where your concentration telescopes toward a still point and you lose awareness of your limbs and the soft shush of your shoe's slide … and whatever's outside the lines of the court, and pretty much all you know then is the bright ball and the octangled butterfly outline of its trail across the billiard green of the court. (18)

The boundaries separating self and other disintegrate, allowing those who experience this "fugue-state" to lose themselves. Instead of thinking, thoughts flow "through" (18) them; things escape their "notic[e]" (18) and "happe[n] very fast but in serial progression" (19).

This "fugue-state" reappears in *Infinite Jest*. Like Wallace, drilling with Gil Antitoi and operating "with the mindless constancy of a machine" ("Tornado Alley" 17), Hal and his peers experience a similar kind of "autonomical" (*Infinite Jest* 117) element of "unconscious exercise [that] becomes a way to escape yourself [and participate in] a long waking dream of pure play" (173). Orchestrated by Gerhardt Schtitt, the morning drills hint at E.T.A.'s curriculum of non-sensation and "egoless[ness]" (110). "Some" are "still asleep on their feet," despite "the mean chill of the dawn" (451). John "Wayne drills with the casual economy of somebody who's in about second gear" (455), suggesting that students are asked to perform these exercises so often that they have become second-nature. But Hal and his classmates do not perform these drills; instead, like the thoughts that use Wallace's young "glabrous" ("Tornado

Alley" 13) body as a conduit for expression (18), the "drills work" (*Infinite Jest* 453), eliminating any need for conscious participation in said exercises at all.

Schtitt's careful leadership ensures a uniform, expected, common experience of the sport. Jim Incandenza, we learn early on, prizes Schtitt's approach so much that he "just about begged [the German] to come on board" (79). For Schtitt, "real tennis" (81) makes "these boundaries of self," in the end, "a game" (82). This central feature—"self-competiti[on]"—is what makes the sport "an essentially tragic enterprise" (84), "[a] matter not of reduction at all but—perversely—of expansion" (82); tennis (as Schtitt conceives it) is a game that features "the true opponent, the enfolding boundary" (84), as "the player himself."

Schtitt hopes the drills will manufacture a "second world inside the world" (459), in which variables like weather (on which Wallace himself so heavily relied during his own junior tennis career) and personal comfort are of no matter. All that matters is only what happens "inside the lines" that mark the court's boundaries; there "is nothing else" (461). At the end of their training session in 9 November Y.D.A.U., Schtitt makes Hal repeat back to him the message of his most recent lecture: "The human head, sir, if I got your thrust … is where I'm going to occur as a player. The game's two heads' one world. One world, sir" (461). This "one world," we can infer, is constituted by the conjoint action of two wills extending themselves into this mutually agreed-upon space, the court, which becomes the place where two people reorganize their realities. The self does not extend beyond its original limits to "escape [it] self." Rather, in E.T.A.'s pedagogy, the self reconstitutes its own boundaries, moving them from their original positions to new ones in order to delineate temporarily a new set of limits—if only for the time it takes to finish a match.

Importantly, self-transcendence is not the goal, even though Schtitt's earlier introductory string of imperatives—"Disappear inside the game: break through limits: transcend: improve: win" (84)—seem to suggest this. What should be transcended is instead *former* limits of the self. Wallace's best description of this concept of self-reconstitution is not, however, in *Infinite Jest*. Instead, we meet a character in his first novel, *The Broom of the System*, who most explicitly endeavors to expand his own boundaries so that he might overcome the devastating solipsism that results from a dichotomous self/other worldview. Norman Bombardini, "an eating fiend of unlimited capacity" (82), is obsessed with what he calls "Project Total Yang" (91), which entails eating literally everything in the universe so that he might somehow evade what he terms "the Great Horror" (90): the prospect of loneliness that accompanies the "self and Other" divide. This division results in a shatteringly "empty, rattling personal universe, one where one finds oneself with the Self, on the one hand, and vast lonely spaces before Others begin to enter the picture at all, on the other." In eating everything in the universe, he hopes to become (as one scholar puts it) "coextensive with the world" (Ryerson 28) by expanding his limits to incorporate the external world, thus transforming the Other into Self through exhaustive circumscription.

In *The Broom of the System*, Bombardini's marginality and absurdity allow us to dismiss the solipsism of early Wittgenstein, a solipsism the mature Wittgenstein himself "roundly reject[s]" (Ryerson 28). But in *Infinite Jest*, the importance of Schtitt's conception of the game as an exercise in reconstructing the self's boundaries is too central to ignore. This "second world" (459) is a reconstituted one, dependent upon the intentional extension of the self into a space with pre-defined boundaries. Jim liked Schtitt so much because the German knew that, as explored above, "the true opponent, the enfolding boundary, is the player himself" (84). What makes tennis such an inherently "tragic and sad and chaotic and lovely" thing is not the loneliness or isolation of playing yourself. Instead, the tragedy lies in the fact that the process of self-reconstitution is infinite, one without end or limit: it is

> an essentially tragic enterprise … [because] you seek to vanquish and transcend the limited self whose limits make the game possible in the first place. … All of life is the same, … the animating limits are within, to be killed and mourned, over and over again. (84)

The "trag[edy]" of this "enterprise" lies not in its endlessness but in what this endlessness prevents. If Schtitt's conception of tennis requires his players endlessly to reconstitute their selves, to push their boundaries outwards to incorporate even the other player against whom they compete, then Schtitt's version of tennis necessarily prohibits self-transcendence. In other words, if Hal and his peers are able continually to redefine their limits, they can never truly transcend themselves. The limits the students do transcend are false limits: as soon as they surpass or "transcend" their boundaries, they can—no, *must*, in order to play Schtitt's tennis—redraw them, thus reinscribing their selves and never extending beyond them into others' worlds.

From this historical passage, we can begin to understand why Jim so prized Schtitt: his own early experiences with the sport were informed by his father's approach towards tennis—an approach almost identical to Schtitt's. On his father's court, the boundaries between subject and object become blurred, allowing the self to move beyond the body and inhabit a reinscribed space. All is within reach for the father's young junior athlete; there are no obstacles because "objects move as they're made to" (166), near-telepathically.

"Susceptible to whim, spin, to force," the tennis ball "will reflect your own character" (165). The talented tennis player in moments of especial promise can occupy a state of expanded consciousness: "The seams and edges of everything" become suddenly tangible (166), and "you play right up to your limit and then pass your limit and look back at your former limit and wave a hankie at it, embarking" (166). This state James describes is one in which the usually clear boundaries of the self become muddled: reality becomes "webbed with nerves" (168), so that even at the outline of the body, "the self … touches all edges" of everything beyond it.

Hal and his peers are at least nominally aware of Schtitt's goal. During a Big Buddy session, Hal tells his charges that "it'll help your attitude"—ease their frustration—"to look for evidence of design" (113). But Hal is not the only one who senses this "coo[l] calculated structure" (114). Leading his own Big Buddy session in a parallel scene, Troeltsch voices what may be the most succinct summary of the Jim/James/Schtitt pedagogical goal: "The court," he declares to his little ones, "may as well be inside you" (118).

2. "Do Not Underestimate Objects!": Wallace and Merleau-Ponty's Phenomenology

If only one concept can be excerpted from *Phenomenology of Perception*, it is that "all consciousness is consciousness *of* something" (27, emphasis mine), meaning that consciousness is intentional, that it always has an object. That this object is sometimes itself, Merleau-Ponty notes, is the fundamental problem with Cartesian mind-body dualism: "As the mediating subject," he writes, "we are never the unreflective subject whom we seek to know" (90). Furthermore, "we are in and toward the world" (14), meaning that "since even our reflections take place in the temporal flow that they are attempting to capture …, there is no thought that encompasses all of our thought." Phenomenology's task, then, is not to explain the "mystery of the world and the mystery of reason" (22) that language mirrors. Its task, rather, is to "*reveal*" (emphasis mine) that self-study is necessarily "infinitely doubled," an inevitable component of "an infinite dialogue or meditation" that, by virtue of the self-reflexivity of the study of consciousness, "will never know just where it is going" (22).

If we can overcome this seemingly endless "self-reflexivity," it is because we can totalize ourselves momentarily to meet the sensory world. "Objective thought is unaware of the subject of perception" (251), Merleau-Ponty declares, meaning that to conceive of oneself as a thinking thing, one must enact a provisional, temporary, and altogether artificial sense of the self as a subject in order to formulate a corresponding predicate. The subject of thought can never be perceived because when the subject turns toward itself, the thing it beholds as its object is but a concept born from a momentary assumption that the thing to which I (as subject) turn is continuous and coherent. Describing the self, then, requires using "an ideal moment of the total act" (262) to verbalize an object. In this way, we always extend beyond any conception of ourselves; that is, in conceiving of ourselves as thinking things, as subjects, we objectify ourselves, which itself entails a kind of duplication: "The consciousness of that which is connected together presupposes the consciousness of that which does the connecting and of its act of connecting" (284). Ultimately, he writes, "I never [can] have an absolute possession of myself by myself" (287).

From this impossibility of total self-possession arises an intriguing predicament. Because we can only conceive of ourselves as objects, not as subjects, we impose artificial limitations on our selves when we enter into thought—and language. To communicate using the word "I" is to indulge in a conceit, to fashion out of an illimitable thing (my being, my self) a provisional place-holding subject by which I can attempt to reach beyond myself and my world. Language, then, mediates not only life but experience of life, too. "It is the very function of language to make essences exist in a separation that is merely apparent, since through language they still rely on the pre-predicative life of consciousness" (16), he writes, meaning that to use language requires a contract of sorts, one by which users must (although usually do not) acknowledge the contingent, provisional, and altogether inadequate nature of language to represent the self.

As we have seen, the manipulation of boundaries is an activity at the very heart of *Infinite Jest*. If tennis is a game that requires its participants to reconfigure the boundaries of their selves so that they can, for at least a brief interval, engage in an activity that allows interaction with others by expansive absorption, it is very much a thing akin to thought and language, which both demand of its users a provisional reconstitution of the self as a clearly delimited thing so that the "I" can enter into the world. At this point, we are left with two very similar questions: Can we ever offer our whole selves to others—or, indeed, to ourselves? And can we ever break out of this continual and infinitely "tragic" rehearsal of boundary-reinscription?

3. *Infinite Jest* as Author's Apology

A joint answer to these questions may lie in James Incandenza's final film, *Infinite Jest*. Reincarnated as a wraith haunting both E.T.A. and poor Gately's fever dream, Jim confesses that

> he spent the whole sober last ninety days of his animate life working tirelessly to contrive a medium via which he and the muted son could simply *converse*. To concoct something that the gifted boy couldn't simply master and move on from to a new plateau. Something that the gifted boy would love enough to induce him to open his mouth and come *out*—even if it was only to ask for more. (838-39, emphases in original)

This "magically entertaining toy," *Infinite Jest* the film, was meant to be "a way to say I AM SO VERY, VERY SORRY and have it *heard*" (839, emphasis in original and text *sic*). But for what was Jim attempting to apologize? Hal has already "fall[en] into the womb of solipsism," just as Jim fears (839): "We're each deeply alone here," Hal laments (112) when he and his classmates are "sit[ting] around and bitch[ing]" (113) about their "common enemy," the E.T.A. program and its administrators. It would seem as if Hal's evaluation of their "common enemy" affords some room for authentic communication and self-transcendence: "[when] we get together and bitch, we're giving something group expression," Hal says, "a community voice" (114). But even this feeling of "community" is orchestrated by the administration, as Hal himself notes, as demonstrated above: there is no "evidence of the tiniest lack of coolly calculated structure." This "community voice" meant to unite is itself evidence of another division among the players because the curriculum is designed to leave room for this outlet of "group expression." That "coo[l] calculated structure" has engendered within Hal an even more profound loneliness, one that cannot be overcome by "sit[ting] around and bitch[ing]." The realization that even in these private moments of communion the curriculum of isolation intrudes is further isolating.

What, then, can soften the kind of loneliness Hal feels so acutely? In his final days, Jim realized there was no way to draw the students out of themselves—and *Hal out of himself*—long enough to realize that this fundamental loneliness the program instills is not all that fundamental. Jim created the film to apologize to Hal for incapacitating him, for founding and subjecting him to an institution that teaches tennis as a way to incorporate other objects as elements of consciousness and not as a way to transcend the illimitable self, to move beyond the boundaries of individual identity and communicate in an authentic fashion with others.

But where Jim seems to fail—not only as filmmaker but also (and this is the more tragic edge) as father as well—Wallace is triumphant, at least in part. Jim's "apology" can be read in two ways. First, it is an expression of sorrow for at least partial responsibility for Hal's nearly crippling solipsism. Secondly, it is an explanation, which is closer to *apology*'s etymological origins that hold that apologies are acts of self-defense, of "speaking away" arguments against the speaker (*OED*).

Wallace's treatment of authorial anxiety and presence elsewhere can help contextualize Jim's failure to communicate sorrow or regret. "Authors are monkeys who mean" (139), quips Wallace in "Greatly Exaggerated," his review of H. L. Hix's *Morte d'Author: An Autopsy*. More than representing mere wit, this statement anticipates Wallace's final conclusion that

> the whole question [of the author's relevance] seems sort of arcane. As William (anti-death) Gass observes in *Habitations of the Word*, critics can try to erase or over-define the author into anonymity for all sorts of technical, political, and philosophical reasons, and "this 'anonymity' may mean many things, but the one thing which it cannot mean is that *no one did it*." (144-45, emphasis in Wallace's quotation of Gass's quoted original)

Merleau-Ponty's phenomenological account of the subjective and subjected self suggests that revealing oneself fully cannot happen in language—the provisional totalization of the thinking subject, represented by his or her use of "I," that language requires necessarily prevents full self-disclosure, given the illimitable nature of being and consciousness—and, thereby, that language is an insufficient medium. Wallace suggests in "Greatly Exaggerated" that traditional poststructuralist declarations of the author's death or insignificance, while well argued, neglect one critical fact: that there is always an individual who is attempting to speak through the text to a reader, the intended recipient of his or her language. Thus the author's failure to "mean" sufficiently because of his or her use of language is not in itself a denial of authority. Given language's inherent inadequacy, even the most adept and shining authors are unable sufficiently to touch their readers.

The significance of the second sense of "apology" becomes more apparent if we interpret Wallace's *Infinite Jest* as an answer to the seemingly unanswerable question that appears to follow from the problems phenomenological subjectivity poses. Is it possible to overcome our situation in language and communicate meaning via some other, less troubled medium? Yes, Wallace answers—and we can still use language to do so. Apologies are, as explicated above, acts of "speaking away." This "speaking away" can be a dismissive act, one by which the speaker can send "away" and thus discharge objections to his or her points. But apologies of this sort also afford the speaker more time to speak on topics different or "away" from his or her presumed one.[1]

Despite his apology's apparent failure (Hal has already fallen into the womb of solipsism), Jim nonetheless succeeds in communicating something. Though his apology never reaches Hal—at least during Y.D.A.U., if not the entirety of the novel—something of his apology reaches us. Wallace authors Jim's apology as a way to "speak away" from Hal, the film's sole intended viewer, and speak towards us, albeit obliquely. In divining what Merleau-Ponty describes as the author's "significative intention which is not guided by any text" ("Voices of Silence" 46) from Jim's *Infinite Jest*, we can assign a transcendent meaning to Wallace's *Infinite Jest*: that, as Wallace declares in "Greatly Exaggerated," "writing is an *act of communication* between one human being and another" (144, emphasis mine)—and only in this communicative act can we hope to extend beyond ourselves and reach others.

4. "The Consciousness Behind the Text": Divining Wallace's Final Point

The reader-writer relationship is an intimate one, bound not only by language but also by humane interests: "The big distinction between good art and so-so art lies somewhere in the art's heart's purpose, the agenda of the consciousness behind the text" (50). This "consciousness," to which Wallace assigns great responsibility, is the author, who must sacrifice himself for the good of his text:

> Really good work probably comes out of a willingness to disclose yourself, open yourself up in spiritual and emotional ways that risk making you look banal or melodramatic or naive or unhip or sappy, and to ask the reader really to feel something. To be willing to sort of die in order to move the reader, somehow. (50)

Wallace admits that acknowledging the necessity of this little death is "sappy": it "requires a kind of courage I don't seem to have yet" (50-51), a "courage" to

---

[1] Most memorably, the Classical example of this avoidant version of "speaking away" is Plato's *Apology*, in which Socrates is allowed the space not only to refute the capital charges against him—of corrupting the youth—but also to explore the larger significance of criticism, wisdom, and virtue. (Undoubtedly, Wallace would have relished the irony of this piece, or at least of the discrepancy between the *Apology*'s subject matter and our modern notion of "apology": Socrates is notably *un*apologetic about his actions, leading all the more to his jurors' decision to convict him.)

"make … writing more generous and ego-driven" (51). This kind of writing-toward-others is, according to Wallace, the closest we can come to inhabiting another's mind and thus achieving anything close to true communication. Text comes alive through the reader, not through the writer, and in this way fiction can "share its valence with the reader" (40) only through her reading of it. This valence-sharing is a deeply human act, one that for Wallace seems to hold the most communicative promise.

In his essay on Wallace's relationship to Wittgenstein, Patrick Horn maintains that Wallace's response to the "perennial problem of solipsism" (246)—which, he claims, Wallace regards as an eternal obstacle because "the inadequacy of language cannot be overcome" (246)—suffers from a fundamental misinterpretation of Wittgenstein's thought. Wallace, Horn suggests, thought that solipsism could only be "confronted and overcome by producing, at best, haunting moments of sincerity" (251). Through a careful exegesis of *Infinite Jest* and its surrounding texts, our present analysis seeks to expose the invalidity of Horn's assertion that Wallace "fail[ed] to appreciate that what connects us, what has always connected us, to others and to the world is our lives, not language" (262).

Horn's thesis is based upon a radical misreading of the final line of Wallace's short story "Good Old Neon," which, Horn writes, "ends with a sentimentality that is not deluded about what the rational self can provide" (266). Horn asserts that the final phrase, "Not another word," does not admit a limit of language, because "feeling stuck by the limits of language is an illusion" (267):

> Language does not "fail" when Wallace's realer self says to the self with a penchant for endless ironizing, "Not another word." The phrase clearly communicates[.] … Does language fail us when we say, "Words cannot express my gratitude"? Is this a failure of language? Is this a failure to communicate gratitude? No, of course not. And likewise, "Not another word" is not a failure of language on any level. (267)

Horn is correct when he writes that saying "words cannot express my gratitude" does, indeed, express a gratitude beyond measurement and thus "communicate gratitude." But his assumption rests on the idea that this phrase is an admission of gratitude, when this phrase is really an admission that the gratitude one feels is *beyond description*, and, in admitting its indescribability, one admits an infinite gratitude. The speaker must acknowledge her inability to "communicate gratitude"—an inability that is itself rooted in the "failure" of language—in order to "communicate" that very same "gratitude." In assuming that Wallace's "Not another word" is an admission not of language's limits but, rather, of the authentic voice's silencing of the ironic voice, Horn misinterprets Wallace's point: that it is through the very use of language that we defy its failure and deny its limiting power over us. While the attempt at authentic self-expression and self-disclosure is futile because of language's inevitable failure, it is the *attempt* at expression that is itself expressive. In other words, the act of expression serves to communicate the intention of self-expression. In this way, communication is an inherently performative act, [2]one that carries meaning only in its articulation.

Infinite Jest is this articulation. In an interview with Charlie Rose following the 1997 release of *A Supposedly Fun Thing I'll Never Do Again*, Wallace maintained that readers who "like[d] [*Infinite Jest*] because it was funny or it was erudite or it was interestingly fractured" suffered from a fundamental "midunderstand[ing] [of] the book." Wallace instead "wanted it to be extraordinarily sad and not particularly postmodern or jumbled or fractured" at all. To be sure, *Infinite Jest* is full of funny puns and jokes, but these jokes are ornamental. Its primary function, like the *Infinite Jest* Jim created in his final days, was to communicate the near-incommunicable: that we are not alone, despite however closed-off and alone we may ourselves feel. This sentiment—a notably authentic one, so free of the kind of devastating irony Wallace exposes in "E Unibus Pluram" that it surely falls into the category of art that baits "the yawn, the rolled eyes, the cool smile, the nudged ribs, the parody of gifted ironists" (81)— engenders the ultimate irony: the book that has become the best cipher and symbol of hipness and cool is the very same book by which Wallace attempts to escape ironic discourse and write towards something bigger, something better. Thus Time's final tragic joke, this true infinite jest.

---

2 This use of "performative" here is very much indebted to J. L. Austin's concept of the "performative utterance," which he describes as a speech act that is distinguished from other types of utterances by its functionality. One of many "*infinite* uses of language" (1290, emphasis in original), Austin's performative utterances reach beyond the verbal into some other realm of being: "If a person makes an utterance of this sort we should say that he is *doing* something rather than merely *saying* something," he writes, pointing to statements such as bets and christenings as examples of speech that "perform" the very "action[s]" they describe (1291). In *How To Do Things With Words*, he offers his clearest definition of "performatives," writing that these statements "in-dicat[e] that the issuing of the utterance is the performing of an action" (6).

Works Cited

"apology, n." *OED Online*. Oxford University Press, December 2015. Accessed 11 December 2015.

Austin, J. L. *How To Do Things With Words*. Harvard University Press, 1962.

-- -- --. "Performative Utterances." *The Norton Anthology of Theory and Criticism*. 2nd ed. Ed. Vincent B. Leitch. W. W. Norton and Company, 2010. 1289-1301.

Horn, Patrick. "Does Language Fail Us? Wallace's Struggle with Solipsism." *Gesturing Toward Reality: David Foster Wallace and Philsoophy*. Eds. Robert K. Bogler and Scott Korb. Bloomsbury, 2014. 245-70.

Merleau-Ponty, Maurice. *Phenomenology of Perception*. Trans. Donald A. Landes. Routledge, 2012.

Ryerson, James. "Introduction: A Head That Throbbed Heartlike: The Philosophical Mind of David Foster Wallace." *Fate, Time, and Language: An Essay on Free Will*. Columbia UP, 2011. 1-36.

Wallace, David Foster. *The Broom of the System*. Penguin Group, 2004. Print.

-- -- --. "Derivative Sport in Tornado Alley." *A Supposedly Fun Thing I'll Never Do Again*. Little, Brown, and Company, 1997. 1-20.

-- -- --. "Greatly Exaggerated." *A Supposedly Fun Thing I'll Never Do Again*. Little, Brown, and Company, 1997. 138-45.

-- -- --. *Infinite Jest*. Back Bay Books, 2006.

-- -- --. Interview by Charlie Rose. *Infinite Jest: Reviews, Articles, & Miscellany*. N.p., 1997. Accessed 11 November 2015.

The Bad Storks: Dad-diction in *The Dream Songs* and *Infinite Jest*

Daniel Leonard

I'm thinking of a particular man. This man was an author, one with remarkable sensitivity, imagination, and linguistic talent. His major work, which absorbed him for years and propelled him to enduring fame, is a sprawling, stylistically groundbreaking book centered on a thinly veiled author surrogate who struggles with addiction and whose father committed suicide. The man saw himself as an outsider, lacking a PhD yet conducting academic research and teaching in universities. In middle age, he tragically took his own life at a time when his last book, a novel somewhat more optimistic in tone than the major work, was unfinished but complete enough to publish.

I'm thinking of John Berryman.

Berryman's major work of poetry *The Dream Songs* and Wallace's novel *Infinite Jest* both draw on the plot, characters, and themes of *Hamlet*. Both emphasize elements of Shakespeare's play that are emphasized by the psychoanalytic interpretation of *Hamlet* proposed by Freud and developed by Ernest Jones and Jacques Lacan. Most notably, both *DS* and *IJ* make the same alteration to their received material: in these works, the father's death is no longer a fratricide, but a suicide—so the son cannot avenge him. What interest me are the implications of this choice for the protagonist sons in both works.

Before discussing those implications, I should address a few questions: Who is John Berryman? What are *The Dream Songs*? And what is the psychoanalytic interpretation of *Hamlet*?

John Berryman was born in 1914, about fifty years before Wallace. He was a poet associated with the Confessional school who, early in his career, envied the success of his friends Delmore Schwartz and Robert Lowell. His first wife Eileen Simpson, a psychologist, documents this period in her memoir *Poets in Their Youth* and provides a great deal of biographical information and analysis. Berryman rose to prominence in the 1950s for his long poem, "Homage to Mistress Bradstreet," and his subsequent collection *77 Dream Songs* won the

1965 Pulitzer Prize for poetry. He published another three-hundred-some Dream Songs in *His Toy, His Dream, His Rest*, which won the 1969 National Book Award; these two works taken together are known as *The Dream Songs*. He published scholarship on Shakespeare, Stephen Crane, and others. He permitted a long sonnet sequence addressed to a lover—both were married, but not to each other—to be published twenty years after the fact. He taught at the Iowa Writers' Workshop, married three times, struggled with alcoholism and depression, checked in and out of various clinics and institutions, experienced a late-life Christian conversion, and, as he had contemplated and described numerous times beforehand in his writing, jumped from a bridge in 1972 at the age of 57. He left behind the unfinished manuscript for his novel *Recovery*, about an intellectual learning to go through the Twelve Steps of AA in a hospital treatment group—perhaps the first novel by a well-known American author to give such close observation to AA.

It's highly unlikely that Berryman knew anything of Wallace, given that at the time of Berryman's death, Wallace was nine years old, but Wallace knew of Berryman. D. T. Max reports that by the late eighties Wallace had read Lewis Hyde's essay arguing that alcoholism ruined Berryman's *Dream Songs*. And evidently, notebooks of Wallace's on display at the Whitney Museum show Berryman quotes he wrote down while working on *The Pale King*, but I have not yet been able to determine which quotes these are, or from which works.

The Dream Songs consists of 385 sections, each based on a pattern of three six-line stanzas (a kind of "devil's sonnet") with varying rhyme schemes. The syntax is often garbled for the sake of expression, for emphasis, and to create ambiguities or multiple simultaneous readings. Likewise, the pronouns are wildly inconsistent, and the diction and dialect shift rapidly. The poems feel spontaneous; Berryman is known to have written some of them on cocktail napkins. The whole poem, as Berryman explains in a preface to the second volume, "is essentially about an imaginary character (not the poet, not me) named Henry, a white American in early middle age sometimes in blackface, who has suffered an irreversible loss and talks about himself sometimes in the first person, sometimes in the third, sometimes even in the second; he has a friend, never named, who addresses him as Mr. Bones and variants thereof."

Elsewhere he says of the "friend" character, "I use friend in quotation marks because this is one of the most hostile friends who ever lived." Controversially, the friend speaks in a Southern black dialect which operates in tandem with Henry's occasional minstrelsy. The implications of this authorial choice are too elaborate to explore here in greater detail, but we'll note a few related factors for our purposes. First, Henry experiences a persistent persecution complex. As Dream Song 1 describes it, "All the world like a woolen lover once did seem on Henry's side. Then came a departure." Second, his sense of emotional and spiritual alienation leads him to identify with various marginalized groups, but at the same time, his sense of an unbridgeable distance between himself and the Other and his fear of intimacy lead him to hostility in relation to figures which differ from him. Third, he shares many unsavory thoughts, feelings, and actions throughout the work. In Dream Song 29, for instance, he says, "But never did Henry, as he thought he did, / end anyone and hacks her body up / and hide the pieces, where they may be found. / He knows: he went over everyone, & nobody's missing. / Often he reckons, in the dawn, them up. / Nobody is ever missing."

That last line sounds almost like a complaint—who might he hope he wakes up one day to find to be missing? Specifically, who should be missing, but isn't? Henry's father, like Berryman's, shot himself at home when Henry was a pre-teen. We'll examine Henry's feelings about his father in more depth later, but suffice it to say that, although the father's body is hidden, his "pieces" still haunt Henry; they aren't missing yet.

The psychoanalytic interpretation of *Hamlet* stems from a passage in Freud's *Interpretation of Dreams*, where he suggests that Hamlet has an "Oedipal desire for his mother and the subsequent guilt [is] preventing him from murdering the man [Claudius] who has done what he unconsciously wanted to do." The theory was extended by Freud's colleague and biographer Ernest Jones in a book and by Freud's student Jacques Lacan in an essay. The long and short of the theory: Hamlet wanted to kill his father and marry his mother. When another man beats him to it, Hamlet is duty-bound to kill that man, but he can't bring himself to destroy "the man who shows him the repressed wishes of his own childhood realized." Surely there are also other themes in *Hamlet*, and this reading does not explain every element of the work. My interest here is not ultimately to justify and argue for this interpretation, but to see how it is used and transformed by Wallace and Berryman. I'll note, though, a few details of *Hamlet*'s plot that support this reading and bear on *The Dream Songs* and *IJ*.

When Hamlet speaks directly about his father, King Hamlet, it's mostly through idealized and generic descriptions of his kingly virtue, including implicit and explicit comparisons to gods. As Lacan puts it, "Hamlet has no voice with which to say whatever he may have to say about [his father]. He actually chokes up and concludes by saying … that he can find nothing to say about his father except that he was like anyone else. What he means is very obviously the opposite." Hamlet fixates on incest as Claudius's chief offense, far more than the usurpation of the throne or even the murder—and this at a time when the status of a marriage such as Claudius's, the brother of the deceased marrying the widow, as incest was not universal, and even Hamlet's father's ghost has to intervene to remind him that he's become more focused on preventing his mother from being intimate with Claudius than on killing Claudius. Hamlet even causes the deaths of numerous others before he gets around to Claudius. When Hamlet confronts his mother in her bedroom, he strikes out at a figure behind a curtain and kills Polonius, claiming to mistake him for Claudius—but Hamlet had just seen Polonius moments before in another room and would have noticed if he'd entered. As Lacan describes it, Hamlet is mostly incapable of taking action, but he leaps at the first opportunity to strike at someone he can't see, someone in his mother's bedroom. Hamlet remains unable to go through with his revenge murder, berating himself for lacking the gumption, until his mother Gertrude has died—and then, with the possibility of fulfilling his desire nullified, with the ambivalence of his relation to Claudius resolved, and being near death himself, he accomplishes it immediately.

So, that's the theory. A thought experiment: Imagine how the play might be different if King Hamlet's death were a suicide. When the death was a fratricide, Hamlet's guilt was directed to his failure to accomplish a specific action: avenging the death. If the death were a suicide, there'd be no particular response demanded—so the guilt would be free-floating, objectless. Instead of becoming obsessed with this one act and feeling anxious for his failure to perform it, the guilt might spread to his relation to achievement in general, especially traditional, objective achievements that could prove his deservingness of his father's love, his well-adjustedness, and perhaps his mother's affection. He wouldn't need to idealize his father anymore, but without a socially acceptable revenge, he'd have no acceptable conduit for his filial aggression. This could translate into taking out his aggressions on himself through various forms of self-punishment: consigning himself to substance dependency, undermining his own achievements and relationships, and attempting to escape the self through altered experiences of consciousness. This is the case as we find it with Henry and Hal.

As for Hamlet's relation to his mother: Without Gertrude remarrying, no real obstacle would prevent Hamlet from seeking to fulfill the second half of his Oedipal desire, but a healthy dose of repression would prevent him from acting on this wish or realizing he has it. Again, remember that in the play as written, Hamlet doesn't pursue Gertrude; the repression is so strong that it's only once she's dead that he's free to act as society demands. So his relationship to his mother could still include the complex layers of neediness, resentment, and awe it did before. This is the case for Hal and for Henry, but we won't linger on this point.

To return to the father relation: What if Henry and Hal *could* find or invent a ritualistic action that would enable them to express their aggression in a symbolic way? Some particular act that would help them resolve their objectless feelings by creating an adequate metaphor for them, relieving the tension by releasing it into the open?

In remarkably similar ways, they both accomplish this—Henry more wittingly than Hal. It's worth noting that Berryman explicitly acknowledged his affirmation of and debt to the psychoanalytic interpretation of *Hamlet* in his Shakespeare lectures; a friend of his went so far as to say that he "identified personally with the period of Shakespeare's tragedies" and that he tried to "recapture" Shakespeare's experience "by trying to relive it." Let's see what leads up to this accomplishment in *The Dream Songs*.

Henry refers ominously to some horrible secret he has, but he seems incapable of naming it. For example, in "Song 168", he says, "I have a story to tell you which is the worst / story to tell that ever once I heard. / What thickens my tongue? / and has me by the throat? I gasp accursed / even for the thought of uttering that word. / I pass to the next Song:"—and there the train of thought ends. The most famous instance is the first stanza of "Song 29":

> There sat down, once, a thing on Henry's heart
> só heavy, if he had a hundred years
> & more, & weeping, sleepless, in all them time
> Henry could not make good.
> Starts again always in Henry's ears
> the little cough somewhere, an odour, a chime.

Note the cough and the chime: In a few instances, Henry uses language appropriate to a trauma experienced by hearing. In "Song 87", he says, "I only speak of what I hear / and I have said too much"—implying simultaneously that he has heard too much and that he has not been able to say all that he heard. Then again in "Song 128", "They are sympathetic, ears, & hears / more than they should or / did." The simplest explanation for what Henry heard is his father's gunshot, which led Henry to run to the source of the sound and discover his father's body in his parents' bedroom. In Freudian terms, that room would also be the site of the primal scene, where Henry may have overheard his parents' intercourse. He also notes hearing his parents fighting—violence being a child's standard interpretation of the primal scene.

In any case, his trauma leads him to fantasize about digging up graves (sometimes his own) and hacking up the bodies, specifically the heads. In "Song 95", he speaks of temptation "to give oneself over to crime wholly [...] until with trembling hands hoist I my true / & legal ax, to get at the brains. I never liked brains [...] but I will like them now, spooning at you, / my guardian, slowly." This wish reveals itself to be directed at Henry's father in the next-to-last Song of the whole work, number 384. The whole of it is crucial, so let's look at the whole thing:

> The marker slants, flowerless, day's almost done,
> I stand above my father's grave with rage,
> often, often before
> I've made this awful pilgrimage to one
> who cannot visit me, who tore his page
> out: I come back for more,
>
> I spit upon this dreadful banker's grave
> who shot his heart out in a Florida dawn
> O ho alas alas
> When will indifference come, I moan & rave
> I'd like to scrabble till I got right down
> away down under the grass
>
> and ax the casket open ha to see
> just how he's taking it, which he sought so hard
> we'll tear apart
> the mouldering grave clothes ha & then Henry
> will heft the ax once more, his final card,
> and fell it on the start.

Note how by the third stanza Henry ceases to describe himself with ordinary pronouns: he uses a demonic "we" to speak of tearing the grave clothes and a distancing third person to speak of axing the body. It's chilling. This treatment stands out all the more against the numerous Songs in which Henry mourns deeply and thoughtfully for various friends who have died.

To refer back to the notion of a trauma of hearing, and a "chime": Henry's gravesite fantasies are sometimes accompanied by a certain two-word phrase. In DS 97, referring to a tombstone, Henry says, "My slab lifts up its arms // in a solicitude entire, too late." This is followed by a command to "gap your mouth to state" a list of increasingly bizarre and non-lingual nonsense.

And in DS 29, right before saying he never hacked anyone's body up, he says, "Ghastly, / with open eyes, he attends, blind. // All the bells say: too late." (The "he" could be the Oedipally blinded son, but it can simply be the dead father staring back from the grave right before the ax hits his eyes.) So, to recap some elements we've gleaned from Henry's fantasy: digging up his father's body, opening up the head, and hearing the phrase "too late."

Let's turn to Hal. He's also the one who found his father's body after the suicide; and in the same way that Henry longs for indifference, Hal dreams of being a "hero of non-action, the catatonic hero, the one beyond calm." Early in *Infinite Jest* but at the end of its timeline, on page 17, Hal thinks of when "Donald Gately and I dig up my father's head." This event is the off-screen climax of *IJ*, and it gets a fuller description toward the end of the book, in Don Gately's feverish thoughts: "He dreams he's with a very sad kid and they're in a graveyard digging some dead guy's head up [...] the sad kid holds something terrible up by the hair and makes the face of somebody shouting in panic: Too Late." If Wallace was not directly influenced by Berryman in crafting this scene, and if there's no common source I'm oblivious to, then this coincidence is akin to Newton and Leibniz discovering calculus independently of each other at the same time. I can't confirm whether Wallace knew *The Dream Songs* well, but if not, great minds think alike—or at least, great minds with very similar personal backgrounds and psychological makeups working half a century apart employ the same literary materials (the psychoanalytic interpretation of *Hamlet*) to solve the same authorial problem (how a character based on Hamlet can fruitfully address his father's death when it's a suicide) in the same way. Yes, it's true that Hal exhumes his father for the purpose of saving the world, believing there's something very important to retrieve in the head, but recall that JOI's wraith tells Gately how he spent his last days "working tirelessly to contrive a medium via which he and the muted son could simply *converse* ... something the boy would love enough to induce him to open his mouth and come *out*—even if it was only to ask for more." When posing as a professional conversationalist, JOI tells Hal directly about a "priapistic-entertainment cartridge implanted in your very own towering father's anaplastic cerebrum." JOI knew Hal would have reason to retrieve this cartridge. And if he had the great psychological insight his filmmaking career suggests, he may have realized that, for Hal, the symbolic act of breaking his father's skull—reenacting the father's violence to his own head as if it had been performed on him by the son—would be just the thing to open his mouth and save the world for Hal.

Neither character brings himself to say the phrase "too late" aloud; it's received or mouthed, and it takes on weight that suggests multiple meanings. For Hal, it at least means: too late to get the cartridge. For Henry, it refers at least to clocks in general ("all the bells") and funeral bells in particular: too late to do anything you wanted to do with this person or change anything about your relationship to them. In "Song 29", "all the bells" is preceded in the same stanza by mention of a "face a thousand years / would fail to blur the still profiled reproach of"—in less elegant words, it's never late *enough* to stop that face from haunting him; it's too late to prevent the unstoppable haunt from starting. And for the psychoanalysts, it's too late for the son to kill the father himself. These senses of the phrase have their place. But most pivotally, "too late" is the underlying message we seek to receive and be sure of through funeral rites: we move through the stages of grief and come to acknowledge and accept that the past really is past, setting aside the delirious idea that we might still be able to change things and the person might come back. We come to know deep down that it's time to move on, and we put our ghosts to rest. Lacan points out that "in all the instances of mourning in *Hamlet*, one element is always present: the rites have been cut short and performed in secret." Hal and Henry are stuck until they can complete their rites and do so openly. For Hal, this means being attended by Gately and John Wayne to the grave and narrating the experience to readers in the first person; for Henry, this means sharing the experience with his readers and, perhaps, his "friend." The short-term effect on Hal is to bewilder his speech, but to clarify his inner voice. The effect on Henry is to silence him, but by finishing the work that provoked him to speak: after he axes the grave, he gives one more Song to end the book, and that's that.

Let us hope that for these author surrogates, and for their authors, the silence is rest.

———

Works Cited

Berryman, John. *The Dream Songs*. Farrar, Straus and Giroux, 2007.

-- -- --. *Berryman's Shakespeare*. Farrar, Straus and Giroux, 1999. Print.

"David Foster Wallace." Whitney Museum of American Art, www.whitney.org/Exhibitions/2014Biennial/DavidFosterWallace. Accessed 27 July 2016.

"David Foster Wallace and 'Blurbspeak.'" *LARB*, 9 August 2015, www.lareviewofbooks.org/article/david-foster-wallace-and-blurbspeak. Accessed 27 July 2016.

Freud, Sigmund, James Strachey, Anna Freud, Carrie L. Rothgeb, and Angela Richards. *The Standard Edition of the Complete Psychological Works of Sigmund Freud*. London: Hogarth Press, 1900. Print.

Lacan, Jacques. "Desire and the Interpretation of Desire in *Hamlet*." Trans. Jacques-Alain Miller and Hulbert James. *Yale French Studies* 55/56 (1977): 11–52. Web. Accessed 27 July 2016.

Lowell, Robert and John Berryman. *Guggenheim Poetry Reading*. New York: Academy of American Poets Archive, 1963. 88 minutes.

The Darkly Delicious Thing: Explorations of the Gothic in *Infinite Jest*
Melissa Holton

In a 1993 interview, David Foster Wallace explained that "…one of the things about living now is that everything presents itself as familiar, so one of the things the artist has to do now is take a lot of this familiarity and remind people that it's strange" (Kennedy and Polk in Conversations with DFW 19). Wallace was writing *Infinite Jest* at the time, and his emphasis on strangeness opens up the possibility that he was thinking of a key Gothic concept, the uncanny. Freud described it as the familiar rendered unfamiliar. "'Unheimlich,' [is] opposed to 'heimlich' which signifies the cozy-intimate sense of homely. The uncanny describes a sense of estrangement within the home, something threatening, tempting and unknown that lies within the bounds of the intimate" (Fisher). Gothic scholar Lucie Armitt delineates the uncanny specifically as Gothic. Not just unknown or unfamiliar, "the unheimlich requires the ongoing trace of homeliness prior to a…shift, having the effect of turning the familiar into the strange or…turning the cherished notion of privacy into the unsettling notion of secrecy" (226).

Wallace's presentation of the relationship between the self and the body and between the self and others points to the uncanny as a meaningful concern. In fact, several distinct aspects of *Infinite Jest* emphasize the uncanny as well as other seminal Gothic concepts such as abjection, liminality, and the psychological horror that connects them. These foundational ideas connect Gothic concerns to certain characters' development in *Infinite Jest*. Angela Carter, an author of Gothic fiction, illuminates what these foundational ideas do. She maintains that the Gothic "retains a singular moral function—that of provoking unease" (459). Wallace himself offered a similar idea in an interview with Larry McCaffery, saying that "a big part of real art fiction's job is to aggravate this sense of entrapment and loneliness and death in people, to move people to countenance it, since any possible human redemption requires us first to face what's dreadful, what we want to deny" (qtd. in Hering 12). Both authors ask readers to turn and face the strange for moral reasons. How does a work of literature provoke unease? By foregrounding where we readers are complicit in our own unexamined, distorted sense of our own selves, bodies, and relationships, in order to remind us that what we see as outside ourselves (and therefore strange and abhorrent) is actually within. *Infinite Jest*, like the Gothic, seeks to provoke unease and look at the moral and psychological quandaries that arise within it. Jerrod Hogle, in *The Cambridge Companion to the Modern Gothic*, examines the slippery work of trying to "define" the Gothic when he lists several Gothic tropes and argues that "Since the Gothic is a mixture of quite different elements and [is] inherently unstable, some fictions use only partial forms of it, employing several but not all of the…elements alongside very different conventions" (5). Hogle refers to these works as the semi– or near–Gothic.

Gothic theorist Fred Botting explains the Gothic "as the mirror of a baser nature, [arising from] a culture in which pleasure, sensation and excitement come from the thrills of a darkly imagined counter-world, embracing the less avowable regions of psyche, family, and society" (12). This "counter-world" relates, in a certain way, to Wallace's admission that "In dark times, the definition of good art would seem to be art that locates and applies CPR to those elements of what's human and magical that still live and glow despite the times' darkness" (Boswell 17). This connects because the dark world, by this measure, becomes a place of crisis and opportunity for confronting the less avowable in one's identity. Botting views the Gothic as an escape into one's darker self, less avowable/recognized, and also perversely entertaining and enthralling due to the lurid enticements of the "counter world". Wallace allows that the darker world is enticing, but also suggests that it has no moral substance in and of itself merely as a dark side. I will demonstrate how provoking unease in order to "face what's dreadful" while at the same time gaining awareness of what is "human and magical" becomes a viable part of the spectrum of the Gothic project, at least in a semi– or near–Gothic capacity.

Stephen King classifies three levels of horror writing, with the last being "the tale of mere 'revulsion' designed to create repulsion" (qtd.in Bloom 155). His schema reveals a Gothic lens for exploring the abject in *Infinite Jest*. As critic Clive Bloom explains, abjection as "a theory of identity crisis…centers on the body's waste or excessive products" as "forms of defilement from which the reader recoils" (164). Bodily fluids get "constantly symbolically reproduced in horror fiction as 'hieroglyphs' for all our condensed fears. These bodily functions both create and…destabilize the ego" (164). Bloom's concept of the ego's involvement in abjection parallels the "cringe worthy" (yet notable) Latin phrasing over the convent door in James Incandenza's film *Blood Sister: One Tough Nun*, "Contraria Sunt Complementa" (Wallace 713) which end note 298 translates as "We Are What We Revile or We Are What We Scurry Around As Fast As Possible With Our Eyes Averted" (Wallace 1054). Bodily functions and products *cannot* be scurried around, ultimately, since *Infinite Jest* stacks up a mountain of abject details. Word searches reveal that *Infinite Jest* contains 127 references to blood, 98 to urine, 44 to piss, 32 to shit, 8 to turds, 2 to excrement, 63 to spit, 21 to saliva, 16 to puke, 38 to vomit, 86 to sweat, 16 to mucus and pus. Thus, there are at least 551 abject images in *Infinite Jest*. These statistics indicate more specific renderings of repulsion, events where characters are made aware of or simply reveal the otherness of their own bodies.

Spending days detoxing in a library bathroom, Poor Tony Krause realizes that "time had become the shit itself" (Wallace 303). In his awareness of time's passing through him in the form of excrement, he seems to contemplate his body as alien and as physical. He considers his body alien because he's not sure how he's able to produce all of the material, given that he's not eaten anything for days (Wallace 303). Additionally, his body has become merely a "conduit" for a repulsive collection of bodily products. In this abject detox scene, Tony resigns himself to endurance, surrendering to a body that carries on an uncontrollable physical reality. Tony's resignation about his body anticipates Hal's imagined rooms of 'excrement' and 'meat' at the end of the novel as he contemplates meaninglessness and lies prone as a "horizontal object" on the Viewing Room floor (Wallace 900). At this point, Hal's view reduces his existence as an "object" to mere consumption and bodily production, *both* of which fill rooms with meaningless material: death (meat) and waste. These abject scenes express some of *Infinite Jest*'s darkest revelations: the characters' worries that their lives may hold little or no coherent meaning. Tony's and Hal's "condensed fears" abjectly form the repulsive darkness that follows the initial enticement of drug addiction. Both characters contemplate waste (actual and theoretical) and both do so while questioning their humanity.

Addiction is also at the root of a significant abject scene in Don Gately's life. Gately's warped awareness that he and Eugene FAX Fackleman are "cooking up" with and sitting in a pool of their combined urine is as abhorrent and wretched an understanding of the self as Poor Tony's or Hal's. Fackleman's "game" of spitting and allowing the spit to nearly touch the mixed pool of urine before sucking the spit "back up and in" has, Gately thinks, "an intoxicating aura of danger to it. The insight that most people like play-danger but don't like real danger hit Gately like an epiphany" (Wallace 937). Here Wallace acknowledges the power of repulsion to reveal human truths. He thus both "depict[s] this dark world and [illuminates] the possibilities for being alive and human in it" (Boswell 17). In this scene of combined abjection and addiction, Gately's awareness hints at *Infinite Jest* being part of the contemporary Gothic, according to critic Stephen Bruhm who says that "What becomes most marked in contemporary gothic…is the protagonists'… compulsive return to certain fixations, obsessions and blockages"(261).

Functioning in the middle of a Venn diagram of the overtly visceral abject and the more ethereal abstractions of the spectral, skulls and deformed heads surface individually and collectively as reminders of the ways in which the self is vulnerable, decaying, and alien. The skull and head images serve as metonymies for concepts about the self. Wallace uses body distortion such as atypical or atrophied development of skulls and heads to illustrate characters' deeper fears about their own decline or decay, often linked to suicide or other forms of self-harm. His description of the Union of the Hideously and Improbably Deformed underscores a Gothic fear of the distorted body, especially since early Gothic texts (such as Matthew Lewis' *The Monk*) use a veil as a way of hiding the identity or moral decay of certain characters.

Arguably, the most important skull in the work is the one dug up from Himself's grave, the one supposedly buried with the original copy of the Entertainment. The skull functions in a liminal/spectral way, seeming to simultaneously exist and not exist. This instability emphasizes its Gothic nature since the Gothic frequently includes liminal characters. One question we might ask is how Hal and Gately can dig it up out of Himself's grave if the head exploded in the microwave during the felo de se. Would it have been possible to reconstruct the skull for burial? Where and how does Himself's skull exist? Endnote 160 may hold some clues. The cartridge of ETA student Eric Clipperton's suicide is supposed to have been "interred right there with J.O. Incandenza's dead body—yickily enough" (Wallace 1033). The term "dead body" doesn't specify the skull but suggests that the body is intact enough to be considered unified. Also, the Clipperton suicide cartridge being placed with JOI's body connects these two suicides of the head, and implies that both characters played games with death.

Other references to Himself's skull appear in potent yet unstable ways. Some concern Hal and are embedded in layers of narrative, so even a careful reader may be unsure whether or how this skull exists. The instability of JOI's skull is presented in Hal's supposed discovery of JOI's suicide (Wallace 257) and in Gately's "dream" about the "really sad kid" holding "something terrible" (Wallace 934). A closer comparison suggests that Wallace may want his readers to pay attention to whether the skull is intact. Hal recounts how the BPD field pathologist talks to him about the pressure inside his father's skull—"the pressure buildup would have been almost instantaneous. Then he gestured at the kitchen walls. Then he threw up" (Wallace 253). In the scene that Hal recounts to Orin (about "performing" for the grief therapist), Orin explicitly says "let me just ask and then I'll never bring it back up again. You had implied before that what was especially traumatic was that Himself's head had popped like an uncut spud" (Wallace 257). Orin's *understanding* of what he *thinks* Hal *implied* about *what he saw* indicates several layers of distance and its purpose seems Gothic, because the final, gruesome physicality of JOI's suicide only comes out in this mitigated way. These layers seem to reflect Hal's strong desire to distance himself from his direct experience of his father's suicide. The exploded skull is a memento mori (a literal and figurative death's-head) expressing the Gothic theme of confronting the pervasive human tendency to deny death. The skull's liminality gets complicated and emphasized by Gately's "dream" in the hospital where he's with "a very sad kid and they're in a graveyard digging some dead guy's head up and it's really important" (Wallace 934). The ambiguity is sustained by Gately's considering this a dream and by some precisely vague wording that "the sad kid holds *something terrible* up by the hair" (Wallace 934) [emphasis mine]. The "something terrible" is JOI's head, presumably, but the vagueness both suggests and resists the skull's integrity. If it can be held up by the hair, there would be at least a reconstructed skull "unit", but Gately's term "something" suggests that it may not be identifiable and may not have structural integrity. At the beginning of the book, Hal's brief mention of this scene describes "Donald Gately and I" digging up "my father's head" (Wallace 17) which neither confirms nor denies Gately's vague "something" since Hal presumably would know whether or not the skull was reconstructed for burial. Hal may expect it to be intact, but we don't know that's what he finds.

Skull instability also appears in the characters born with soft or missing skulls, people such as the blind tennis player and Marathe's wife, Gertraude. Wallace appears at times to balance the severity of the "compromised" or non-existent skull imagery with a kind of absurdist humor, nearly a mock Gothic tone. When discussing *Infinite Jest* with David Lipsky, Wallace admitted that he liked "a joke that you laugh hard at, but then it's sort of unsettling, and you think about it for a while. It's not quite black humor, but it's a kind of…creepy humor" (Lipsky 272).

Dymphna, the blind kid, the "infantile native" from Ticonderoga NNY who "evacuated too late" and thus had "several eyes in various stages of evolutionary development in his head but was legally blind" is specifically mentioned as "still an extremely solid player" in the same sentence as his skull which "was apparently the consistency of a Chesapeake crabshell" (518). Gothic critic Jerrold Hogle defines horror as "visible violence, dismemberment, and death" but sees terror as "the frightened anticipation of potential but uncertain threats" (5). Literary historian Sue Chaplin points out succinctly that from the Gothic's "inception…the mutability and monstrosity of the body" has been a key concept (233). The potentiality of "several latent eyes" inside Dymphna's head indicates a Gothic sense of the body. Chaplin refers to the "perverse physicality"(247) of the Gothic's sense of the body, and this perversion (seen in the soft and missing skulls in *Infinite Jest*) leads easily to critic Jeffrey Jerome Cohen's assertion that "'[Monsters] are disturbing hybrids whose externally incoherent bodies resist attempts to include them in any systematic'" structure (qtd. in Chaplin 249). This is seen most notably in the Creature in *Frankenstein*. The several eyes and crabshell skull compare to the perverse physicality of the Creature's assembled corpse parts. This external incoherence of the physical body repeats throughout *Infinite Jest*, perhaps most jarringly in characters whose skulls are missing, such as Remy Marathe's wife Gertraude.

Both Dymphna and Gertraude are mutants, surviving thanks to medical paraphernalia and the kindness of others. What makes their physical selves gothic is not merely their mutations, but the abject and uncanny *descriptions* of the mutations. Both characters' mutated eyes are described in a matter of fact tone that strangely heightens the Gothic effect. The uncanny strikes us when we think carefully about how both characters use realistic medical appliances for their freakish mutations. Deliberate vagueness lurks in Wallace's image of "several eyes in various stages of evolutionary development" (Wallace 518); the imprecise word "several" and the nonchalant tone of the word "various" emphasize the complexity of the genetic freakishness by implying that it's too horrific to pinpoint more precisely. The abject emerges when the blithe tone is combined with these "externally incoherent" Gothic grotesque bodies.

Another prominent gothic trope is the use of liminal beings. Liminality is an in between state of existence, but in the Gothic it takes on a particularly spectral meaning, referring to beings that seem both living and dead, hallucinatory and physically/materially real. JOI, of course, appears doubly liminal as a wraith who may also be a hallucination. Another liminal being is the creepy face in the floor that Hal sees. Its liminality gets underscored by its appearance as both dream and waking hallucination. Hal all but declares this nightmarish face as specifically Gothic and uncanny when he thinks of "a sensation that can be felt asleep or awake…the sudden intra-dream realization that the nightmare's very essence and center has been with you all along, even awake; it's just been overlooked; and then that horrific interval between realizing what you've overlooked and turning your head to look back at what's been right there all along, the whole time" (Wallace 61–62). The lack of a discrete asleep or awake condition signifies that the horror is ubiquitous, intimate, and personal. It heightens the liminality. In his book *Elegant Complexity*, Greg Carlisle suggests that the face in the floor appears to be discussed by an unidentified first person narrator and may be "meant to signify the universality of nightmares at ETA or to signify that more than one ETA dreamer sees the face in the floor" (59). If the face indicates a shared fear among the ETA students then it may, in a way, appear to have a kind of supernatural or at least communal agency that would otherwise be limited/checked. The face may not be tied to one person's psyche/fears, even though it might appear to the individual character as having come out of themselves *individually*. By blurring this line between the personal and the communal, Wallace accesses what gothic terror tries to accomplish—revealing in a vague enough way what psychological horror looks like so that it can continue to be imagined mysteriously.

In a communal manner echoing the hallucination of the face in the floor, a few characters offer a frightening image of a black wing as emblematic of the horror of their depression. The dark shape becomes active and rises inside Geoffrey Day to the point where he says that "It is the most horrible feeling I have ever imagined, much less felt. There is no possible way death can feel as bad" (Wallace 650). There too is the uncanny intimate sense of the terror's having been with Day (and Kate Gompert, to whom he's speaking) all along, like the face in the floor's sense of the terror's being personal, and inevitable, coming out of one's self. As Day confesses, "And there was this idea underneath that you'd brought it on, that you'd wakened it up…. You despised yourself for waking it up" (Wallace 650). Its liminal/seeming nature comes into focus when we pay attention to the amorphous descriptions: "the triangular horror"; repetition of the reference to the black wing with the word it; "hell itself"; "that black sail or wing"; "Time in the shadow of the wing of the thing too big to see, rising" (Wallace 650–651). The black shape is understood deeply and intuitively, but in a way that seems spectral, less visceral/abject than the other near–Gothic horrors in *Infinite Jest*, but not in a weaker or somehow less horrific way. The billowing black wing imagery is liminal and amorphous precisely because the horror brought on by the suicidal level of depression necessitates abstract language. As seminal Gothic author Horace Walpole says in *The Castle of Otranto*—"words cannot paint the horror" (22).

What makes the Gothic lens work for *Infinite Jest* is that, in addition to the portrayals of horror, the abject, and the liminal, Wallace uses these concepts in a way that is fully his. His book is perversely funny, uniquely terrifying, and profoundly sad, sometimes simultaneously. The value of the Gothic lens is that it offers a way to discover and discuss the darkest and creepiest aspects of *Infinite Jest* as part of a semi– or near–Gothic tradition, but it also offers a fresh view of the book's achievements. Where Wallace's work appears to diverge from at least some Gothic literature is that his narrative fosters an intimacy with the reader that reminds us that we are not confronting this darkness alone. Wallace's work is a treasure trove of darkly delicious things, ones which entice us, haunt us, and remind us that our inner darkness is worth confronting and redeeming.

Works Cited

Armitt, Lucie. "The Gothic and Magical Realism." *The Cambridge Companion To The Modern Gothic*. Ed.Jerrold E. Hogle. Cambridge UP, 2014. 224–239.

Bloom, Clive. "Horror Fiction: In Search of a Definition." *A Companion To The Gothic*. Ed. David Punter. Blackwell Publishing, 2001. 155–166.

Boswell, Marshall. *Understanding David Foster Wallace*. U of South Carolina P, 2003.

Botting, Fred. "In Gothic Darkly: Heterotopia, History, Culture." *A Companion To The Gothic*. Ed. David Punter. Blackwell Publishing, 2001. 3–14. Bruhm, Steven. "The Contemporary Gothic: Why We Need It." *The Cambridge Companion To Gothic Fiction*. Ed. Jerrold E. Hogle. Cambridge UP, 2002. 259–276.

Carlisle, Greg. *Elegant Complexity: A Study of David Foster Wallace's* Infinite Jest. Sideshow Media Group, 2007.

Carter, Angela. *Burning Your Boats: The Collected Short Stories*. Penguin Group, 1995.

Chaplin, Sue. *Gothic Literature*. York Press, 2011.

Fisher, Shahar. "Sigmund Freud—'The Uncanny'—Summary and Review." *The Cultural Reader*. 23 February 2014. Accessed 2 June 2016.

-- -- --. "The Uncanny/Unhomely in Bhabha's 'The World and The Home'." *The Cultural Reader*. 27 March 2014. Accessed 2 June 2016.

Hering, David, ed. *Consider David Foster Wallace*. Sideshow Media Group, 2010.

Hogle, Jerrold. "Introduction: Modernity and the Proliferation of the Gothic." *The Cambridge Companion To The Modern Gothic*. Ed.Jerrold E. Hogle. Cambridge UP, 2014. 1–19.

Kennedy, Hugh and Geoffrey Polk. "Looking for a Garde of Which to Be Avant: An Interview with David Foster Wallace." *Conversations With David Foster Wallace*. Ed. Stephen J. Burn. Jackson: UP of Mississippi, 2012. 11–20.

Lipsky, David. *Although Of Course You End Up Becoming Yourself*. Broadway Books, 2010.

McCaffery, Larry. "An Expanded Interview with David Foster Wallace." *Conversations With David Foster Wallace*. Ed. Stephen J. Burn. UP of Mississippi, 2012. 21–52.

Walpole, Horace. *The Castle of Otranto with William Bedford: Vathek and Thomas Love Peacock: Nightmare Abbey*. Wordsworth Editions Limited, 2009.

Wallace, David Foster. *Infinite Jest*. Back Bay Books, 1996.

Who's There? I Am:
Ghosts and Intertextuality in *Infinite Jest*
Melissa Newfield

Subtle nods to Shakespeare's *The Tragedy of Hamlet, Prince of Denmark* populate David Foster Wallace's 1996 novel, *Infinite Jest*. These allusions also seem to extend to the critical work done about *Hamlet*. Because so many of these connections exist, I choose to examine three themes in particular as they are presented in connection with *Hamlet* in Roland Mushat Frye's *The Renaissance Hamlet: Issues and Responses in 1600* (1984) and are also to be found in *IJ*: mourning, incest, and most importantly, the centrality of the ghost to the work.

Frye's work looks at *Hamlet* through the lens of the values and morals of Renaissance England. Two issues Frye develops that become especially provocative when paired with a reading of *IJ* are mourning and incest. These are concepts that have changed over the centuries, and Wallace seems to consciously include them in his own work, while updating them to make sure to trigger reactions from his audience. Frye also discusses how King Hamlet's ghost is widely hailed among *Hamlet* critics as the central literary element and the catalyst for action in the play. Similarly, the ghost of James Orin Incandenza (J.O.I., Himself) is the father-figure in *Infinite Jest*; he also has his existence called into question and instigates a great deal of doubt and confusion even as he dominates the novel through his actions.

Appropriate mourning is one topic Wallace takes up on behalf of *Hamlet*. Frye relates that in the

> Renaissance, ceremonies were not regarded as merely superficial observances, but rather as contributing to and even in some sense insuring the good health of society. So here: properly observed forms and protocols of funeral and mourning were necessary to the health of the surviving family and friends and, especially within the royal family. (82)

Being in mourning included but was not limited to, especially for the court, wearing special garments, somber observances, lack of open gaiety, and the use of special objects. For the spouse of a deceased, mourning was observed more strictly and included not remarrying within a certain amount of time. The outward appearance of a person in mourning and the time spent grieving were definitely factors in the way Elizabethans would perceive that person. Hence, in *Hamlet* something could be said to be "rotten in the state of Denmark" because it was observably so due to the lack of moral conventions being performed satisfactorily by the royal family (I.iv).

Hamlet finds himself in the midst of a morally corrupt situation, and he wants to set the kingdom right again. So, in Act I, when the court meets and Claudius chides Hamlet for being in mourning still, the king is *very much in the wrong*, socially speaking. Claudius asks Hamlet, "How is it that the clouds still hang on you?" To this, Hamlet replies, "Not so, my lord, I am too much i'th' sun" (I.ii.66–7). Hamlet means that this court is behaving much too lightly after the recent death of his father. Then, the new king makes a scandalous pronouncement for the time, even implying that Hamlet's mourning his father a few months after his death is somehow not masculine:

> 'Tis sweet and commendable in your nature, Hamlet,
> To give these mourning duties to your father:
> But, you must know, your father lost a father;
> That father lost, lost his, and the survivor bound
> In filial obligation for some term
> To do obsequious sorrow: but to persevere
> In obstinate condolement is a course
> Of impious stubbornness; 'tis unmanly grief. (I.ii.87–94)

Mourning for the death of the former king should have lasted much longer, yet under the rule of Claudius, the entire Danish Court seems to be suffering from a forgetful delusion. This collective social *faux pas* includes the other characters like Ophelia, Laertes, Polonius, Rosencrantz and Guildenstern, and anyone else in Elsinore not still mourning the old King Hamlet. However, Gertrude, Claudius, and any other relative such as Hamlet, were most closely bound to wear the most somber of garments and participate in solemn, contemplative activities in memory of the deceased. Yet, in Act I they are clad in gay wedding fineries, the wedding of Claudius and Gertrude having taken place "within a month" (I.ii.153). Frye says Claudius should have remained in black for several months, minimum, and Gertrude should have mourned at least a year, maybe more, depending on Danish social customs, which Frye indicates are even more conservative than British (83–5). However, we know Hamlet has been summoned back to the Netherlands for his father's funeral, yet "two months … nay not so much, not two" (I.ii.138) later, Hamlet cannot believe he is also there for the wedding of mother and uncle. He spouts "Thrift, thrift. The funeral baked meats/ Did coldly furnish forth the marriage tables," implying that the grieving time was so short between the events that the same food was used (I.ii.179–80). The general practice of international mourning on behalf of Himself bears mentioning because it directly links to the mourning Frye describes during Elizabethan times.

In contemporary America and in *Infinite Jest*, mourning has changed, but the topic is still present in the narrative. J.O.I. is so important that he was mourned internationally as well as by the members of his profession, family, and Enfield Tennis Academy. The reader finds out fairly early in the novel that

> Professor James O. Incandenza, Jr.'s untimely suicide at fifty-four was held a great loss in at least three worlds. President J. Gentle… conferred a posthumous citation and conveyed his condolences… Certain young quote 'apres-garde' and 'anticonfluential' filmmakers employed, in their output for the Year of the Trial-Size Dove Bar, certain oblique visual gestures—most involving the chiaroscuro lamping and custom-lens effects for which Incandenza's distinctive deep focus was known—that paid the sort of deep-insider's elegiac tribute no audience could be expected to notice. An interview with Incandenza was posthumously included in a book on the genesis of annulation. And those of E.T.A.'s junior players whose hypertrophied arms could fit inside them wore black bands on court for almost a year. (65)

Similar to mourning in Elizabethan times, wearing black and dedicating certain actions are employed as tokens to the memory of the deceased. Wallace's attention to these details certainly solidifies *Jest*'s connection to *Hamlet* and its narrative and to Frye's revelations about the moral content of Shakespeare's Danish tragedy.

In another example, Hal's brother, Mario Incandenza, sparks a late-night discussion with Hal over the lack of tears from his own mother, Avril Incandenza, on behalf of J.O.I. (40). This conversation smacks of the same concerns Hamlet voices in soliloquy in Act I. Hamlet says, bitter even before meeting the ghost of his father and learning the full implications of the murder, that "a beast that wants discourse of reason/ Would have mourned longer!—married with mine uncle,/ My father's brother … within a month,/ Ere yet the salt of most unrighteous tears/ Had left the flushing of her gallèd eyes" (I.2. 150–55). Wallace also examines the idea of crying to indicate grief. However, Wallace makes a point to add several references as to how appropriately Avril Incandenza (the Moms) and to a lesser degree, his maternal half uncle, Charles Tavis (half- or step-brother of Avril) had mourned. Mario wonders, similar to Hamlet above, how her brand of crying betrays her lack of grief. Mario says to Hal, "How come the Moms never cried when Himself passed away? I cried, and you, even C.T. cried. I saw him personally cry … You listened to Tosca over and over and cried and said you were sad. We all were." Mario then asks, "Hey Hal, did the Moms seem like she got happier after Himself passed away, to you … It seems like she got happier. She seems even taller. She stopped travelling everywhere for this or that thing … How come she never got sad?" Hal answers Mario, "She did get sad, Booboo. She just got sad in her way instead of yours and mine. She got sad, I'm pretty sure." He reminds Mario about the flags lowered to half-mast "out front by the portcullis" after the loss and annually at Convocation to remember J.O.I. and says that there are two ways one can bring a flag to half-mast. One is to lower the flag, and the other is to "raise the pole to like twice its original height" (41–2). This parable is meant to be Hal's concession as to how Avril grieves.

In another important conversation between Hal and his other brother, Orin Incandenza (O), Orin assaults Hal with questions about J.O.I.'s death and the surrounding circumstances. Orin implies that the Moms and C.T had probably moved too fast to certain courses of action. O supposedly wants clarification for an upcoming interview with *Moment* magazine featuring the entire family. Orin hadn't been there for the suicide or the funeral of their father, so he has to ask Hal about the events. Hal had been the one to find his father dead with his head stuck in the microwave. The conversation is filled with references to the appropriateness of the grieving processes.

O first wants to know if Tavis, who is implied to be Avril's sometime lover, had moved into the Headmaster's Quarters next to Avril before or after the suicide. Hal answers, "Immediately before. Two, three days before. C.T. had had what's now de Lint's room, next to Schtitt's in Comm.-Ad." Orin reacts with another question about whether "Dad knew they were …?" To this, Hal replies, "Very close? I don't know, O." (247). O's question implies that Orin had known about Avril's indiscretions with Tavis and he wonders if Hal knew/knows.

Orin then wonders who "keeps [Himself's] memory alive, verbally, the most now: [Hal], C.T., or the Moms?" Hal admits that Mario talks with all of them about J.O.I., although they don't bring it up and only talk about it with Mario. Perhaps in reference to the question, which almost seems to be read from a form, a few moments later, Hal says to Orin, "You know, why don't you go ahead and ask me whatever standard ghoulish questions you want…. This may be your only shot. Usually I seem not to talk about it" (248–9).

O expresses quasi-concern over the mourning process Hal went through when he states that Hal "must have been traumatized beyond fucking belief." Hal says yes, and that as a result "the Moms had begun interviewing top-flight trauma- and grief-counselors … within hours after it happened" and that he "was shunted directly into concentrated grief- and trauma-therapy" located right down the road from E.T.A. (252). Hal reveals that grief therapy made him anxious because he was unable to satisfy this therapist with conventional tactics. Hal took to studying books on the grieving process in order to convince the counselor that he had grieved adequately. Eventually, Hal relates to his brother how he had become consumed with anxiety over the situation, or as he tells Orin, "I'd become obsessed with the fear that I was somehow going to flunk grief therapy" (254).

The described situation comes to a head when Hal begins losing his tennis rank and sleep over not being able to satisfy this counselor on having grieved sufficiently, which, ironically, the counselor takes as Hal *beginning* to grieve sufficiently. Exasperated, Hal turns to the study of not the books about the process of grief but the books for the therapists of grief, the books for *professionals*. Armed with this new knowledge, Hal attends a session under the guise that he is angry at the therapist and "accused the grief-therapist of actually inhibiting" his own grieving process.

Not getting the idea that Hal had been faking this experience, Orin wonders, though if Hal "got through it" and whether he "grieved to everybody's satisfaction" (255). Hal responds with a final story about finding his father. He had been practicing and playing hard all afternoon. J.O.I. had rigged the microwave to basically cook his head. Since Hal had been hungry after that afternoon's tennis matches, he tells both Orin and the grief therapist that when he smelled the cooked head first not knowing what it was, that it made his mouth water. He had shrieked at the therapist that "it wasn't [his] fault … *That something smelled delicious!*" (256).

Orin is just as taken in by the story as the therapist had been. However, Hal actually felt little or no emotion and had merely faked anger and his macabre hunger to "pass" grief therapy. This conversation shows that since the youngest Incandenza wasn't capable of bringing actual emotions into this therapy or the conversation with Orin, Hal had to put the situation into a context in which he could control—grades. The story serves the dual purpose of satisfying the same kind of "ghoulish" questions for Orin that it had for the therapist. What had happened in the moments when Hal discovered his dead father? How was Hal upset by this? How did the grieving go? Both Orin and the therapist seem satisfied with the answers they receive, while Hal can return to his life at the tennis academy without the pressure of these unanswered questions hanging over his head. He had passed both inquisitions.

Mourning or the formal process of grieving was extremely important to the people of the Renaissance and to *Hamlet*'s audience. Frye's emphasis of the lack of observance for this moral convention in *Hamlet* is there to remind the reader that contemporary audiences have misunderstood that aspect of the play. In an attempt, perhaps, to keep people from glossing over the same aspect of his novel, Wallace deliberately makes the reader aware that James Orin Incandenza was a figure worthy of being remembered internationally as well as locally. Furthermore, Wallace emphasizes that even though J.O.I.'s sons are still coming to terms with his grisly suicide over four years later, his own wife has not acknowledged his passing with the respect it deserves.

Curiously, another intertextual aspect Frye mentions alongside mourning which can be developed in conjunction with *Hamlet* and *Infinite Jest* is that of incest. Today, marrying one's in-law who has been widowed might seem less scandalous than in times past. In *The Renaissance* Hamlet, Frye explains how in Shakespeare's time, marrying one's brother- or sister-in-law was not just "frowned upon" or curious, it was considered incest. Frye writes that the "marriage of brothers- and sisters-in-law had been branded shameful over hundreds of years of moral teaching since Old Testament times" (77). Some form of the word "incest" occurs several times in *Hamlet*. The first is a famous line from Hamlet's earliest soliloquy, before he knows the extent of the treachery of his mother and uncle: "O most wicked speed, to post/ With such dexterity to incestuous sheets! It is not, nor it cannot come to good" (I.ii.156–8). Later, when Hamlet meets his father's ghost, the ghost calls Claudius, "that incestuous, that adulterate beast" (I.v.42). The ghost begs Hamlet to "Let not the royal bed of Denmark be/ A couch for luxury and damnèd incest" (I.v. 82–3).

While no taboo exists like the one placed on Elizabethan in-laws today, Wallace creates an incestuous situation with his Gertrude character, yet escalates it so as to almost certainly be viewed as morally offensive by contemporary audiences. Wallace takes the implications of incest even further by making Mario seem to be the illegitimate child of Avril and Charles, who may be Avril's half-brother. As the text indicates, "Headmaster, Dr. Charles Tavis, a Canadian citizen, [is] either Incandenza's half-brother or adoptive brother, depending on the version" (81). Wallace wanted to make sure that the audience views the relationship between C.T. and Avril as incestuous, confirming the idea in a later passage revealing through the flexible third-person omniscient narrator that Tavis suspects that the deformed Mario might be his son. Mario has fallen asleep on the floor and Tavis "can feel the mean chill of the dawn just outside ... the thing it's not entirely impossible he may have fathered asleep up next to the sound system with its claws on its chest and four pillows for bradypnea-afflicted breathing" (451).

Wallace takes the incestuous Gertrude figure even further by implying that she might have also committed incestuous acts with Orin and certainly that she fantasized about them. Oldest of the three Incandenza sons, Orin is the hardest on Avril. He has completely physically separated himself from the Moms and, therefore, the rest of the family. He no longer speaks directly to her and didn't speak to Hal for two years after his father's death. So, Orin's criticisms come mostly via the phone conversations between him and Hal. Interestingly, though, Avril is shown to miss her son Orin to a perverse degree that matches up with twentieth and twenty-first century readers' reinvention of the promiscuous and incestuous Gertrude figure from *Hamlet*. Avril is found having sex with E.T.A. senior John Wayne by student, Michael Pemulis, on page 552. In this scenario, Wayne is wearing football pads and a jockstrap, and Avril is dressed like a cheerleader—a sexual parody of Orin and his first and only serious girlfriend, Joelle Van Dyne's, initial relationship.

While incest isn't depicted in quite the same way in *Infinite Jest*, it is one of the moral and social issues from *Hamlet* that Wallace has imbedded in the text. Frye points out that while contemporary *Hamlet* audiences may simply miss or ignore these issues, Elizabethans would have recognized them and found them controversial. In *Jest*, so much information generally exists, that these social matters can be obfuscated by it. However, the many nuances Wallace presents of this particular issue would suggest that he wanted this connection with *Hamlet* to remain strongly present.

Perhaps the most important connection Wallace makes with Frye's ideas pertains to the centrality of the ghost to the text. King Hamlet's ghost is the catalyst for the action of the tragedy; similarly, Incandenza's wraith has already caused certain paradigms to exist because of his work in annular fusion and his creation of the deadly *Infinite Jest* cartridge being pursued in the novel. Wallace updates the ghostly aspect of *Hamlet* in a way that closely mirrors it. *Infinite Jest* can be viewed largely as a ghost story just as *Hamlet* can.

Critics of Shakespeare's *Hamlet* have long had a special interest in the ghost and his ambiguous intentions. Nearly every work dealing with the play has something to say about the mystery behind the ghost of King Hamlet. Drawing

from the text, during Act I, Hamlet articulates the following conundrum:
> Be thou a spirit of health or goblin damn'd,
> Bring with thee airs from heaven or blasts from hell,
> Be thy intents wicked or charitable,
> Thou com'st in such a questionable shape
> That I will speak to thee. (I.vi 40–44)

In the most basic of terms, Hamlet does not know whether the spirit is evil or good, and Elizabethan audiences would have recognized this conflict before Hamlet spelled it out, as Nigel Alexander notes in *Poison, Play, and Duel: a Study in* Hamlet (1971) (31). Both Alexander and Frye mention this characteristic in connection with King Hamlet's ghost. Alexander writes, "Doubt and uncertainty surround every appearance of the Ghost" (30). Similarly, Frye posits that the "Ghost not only launches the action of the tragedy, but in doing so he confronts the Prince with a dangerous task and also with uncertainty and enigma" (14). The ghosts of *Jest* and *Hamlet* both have cryptic and indeterminate natures. In *Jest*, every character confronted with varying degrees of evidence of J.O.I. seems confused or upset. The wraith moves objects of the living: E.T.A. student Ortho Stice's bed, the cook's equipment, Himself's own camera are all found in circumstances that trigger anxiety and sometimes panic in those people who find them. Recovering addict, Don Gately, is the character who we see most closely communicate with the ghost; the ghost seems to try to overwhelm Gately with proof that he exists.

One possibility in the minds of the first *Hamlet* audiences, according to Frye, might be that the ghost of King Hamlet is not real, that he is a figment of the imagination of the night watchmen who originally encounter him. Shakespeare goes to deliberate means to prove that the ghost *is* real by first having Horatio, Hamlet's friend, a thinker and skeptic, take the ghost seriously. Wallace also installs a few assurances that the wraith of Incandenza is a viable character in the novel. The important section containing the "ghostwords" is a part of a dreamy-hallucinatory portion with Don Gately recovering from a gunshot wound while refusing all relief of opiate painkillers. These words are part of J.O.I's (and Wallace's) campaign to prove the existence of the wraith to Gately, who is trapped in a hospital bed and prone to hallucinations. Wallace features a ghost so much smarter than the person (Gately) he communicates with that the reader understands much more about what the wraith communicates to him than Gately when the wraith forces a list of what Gately thinks of as "ghostwords" into his mind (884).

The words start on 832 and are in all capital letters, possibly implying that as they are forced in, the words seem shouted. Gately is a recovering addict in immense pain trying not to get "dosed" with painkillers as he recovers from a gunshot wound. Gately doesn't recognize or understand the words. This ignorance provides proof for Gately and for the reader, as we understand the words through the wraith's intrusion on Gately's "like brain-voice" and through a slippery third-person omniscient narrator even as Gately realizes that he doesn't know them—before the intrusion of the wraith, they simply didn't exist for him.

With this interaction, surely, Wallace was playing with the idea of the actual definition of "ghost words," or words that are accidentally included in a dictionary or other important work and are therefore born into a kind of non-existence or temporary existence. Friday, 21st May, 1886, Professor and Reverend Walter William Skeat of the Philological Society delivered an address to the members and president of his society coining the term "ghost words." He gives the example of "abacot"; this was a non-existent word "defined by Webster's as 'the cap of state formerly used by English kings wrought into the figure of two crowns.'" This submission was then rejected by OED editor when a decision was to be made whether or not to put it in the comprehensive dictionary. The non-existent term was blundered into existence by a mistake. These terms, as Skeat says quite eloquently, he "takes leave to call ... 'ghost-words.' Like ghosts we may seem to see them; when we would do so, they disappear" (352). This definition may fit with the idea that when Gately examines the words the ghost forces into his mind they don't exist in the sense of actually knowing what they mean. Perhaps they disappear from his mind just as quickly as they come.

The ghost appears to Gately among other surreal visions, pain-induced deliria, and feverish dreams from which Wallace will use the ghostwords to distinguish J.O.I. Initially, or for a first-time reader, the presence of the wraith might get lumped in with the stories of the stream of visitors Gately is bound to, listening in his hospital bed. The wraith begins attempting to convince Gately that he is being visited by a ghost—as opposed to the feverish dreams and visions. In order to do so, the wraith seems to be "showing off" in some ways. The ghost first provides the explanation about his own exceptionality as a wraith to Gately, or as he says, wraiths are not generally able to sit still long enough to converse with living humans. He also brings Gately an Asian Coca-Cola can and a picture of crooner-turned-President, Johnny Gentle, from Gately's bunk at Ennet House Recovery House. Then, in quite a dramatic turn, the ghost begins spinning around the hospital room, perhaps in wild demonstration of the word, "PIROUETTE", which Gately suddenly finds in his mind.

> The narrator relates that besides PIROUETTE,
> Other words and terms Gately knows he doesn't know from a divot in the sod now come crashing through his head with the same ghastly intrusive force, e.g. ACCIACCATURA and ALEMBIC, LACTRODECTUS MACTANS and NEUTRAL DENSITY POINT, CHIAROSCURO and PROPRIOCEPTION and TESTUDO and ANNULATE and BRICOLAGE and CATALEPT and GERRYMANDER and SCOPOPHILIA and LAERTES—and all of a sudden it occurs to Gately the aforethought EXTRUDING, STRIGIL and LEXICAL themselves—and LORDOSIS and IMPOST and SINISTRAL and MENISCUS and CHRONAXY and POOR YORICK and LUCULUS and CERISE MONTCLAIR and then DE SICA NEO–REAL CRANE DOLLY and CIRCUMAMBIENTFOUNDDRAMALEVIRATEMARRIAGE. (832)

On page 836, Gately tries not to think of the "cold total ache on his whole right side—DEXTRAL." 862 finds Gately sitting with Joelle, when he suddenly gets the idea to grab her and mimes the movement of a pen, but he worries about grabbing her because he is not left-handed, which "is to say SINISTRAL." On 884, he returns to some of the unknown words now in his mind, repeating, again, SINISTRAL, and adding LIEBESTOD and OMMATOPHORIC. These words are selected by J.O.I. in particular to prove to Gately that the wraith might have a serious agenda as opposed to the cathartic stories other visitors have told Gately while he can't move or talk.

Not much has been written on these words and *Infinite Jest*. In 2003, Jonathan Goodwin wrote a short article called "Wallace's *Infinite Jest*" and was the first to focus on the ghostwords. He writes that

> As Gately wonders if he is dreaming or hallucinating, a series of words and phrases race into his consciousness. These "ghostwords," which Gately does not know "from a divot in the sod" (832) recapitulate Incandenza's life. The capitalized series of obscure terms are mainly medical or optical in origin. (122)

Goodwin concludes that "which is most hidden is often most important" where these ghostwords are concerned. Truly a fruitful topic for future scholarship, consideration of these words includes much central to approaching an understanding of Wallace's novel; they contain *Hamlet* references, film and art terms, father-son dynamics, the idea of language itself, scientific vocabulary, and things pertinent to Gately's own life.

After Gately is more willing to believe in the wraith's existence, he finds out the ghost actually intends to talk about his relationship to his own sons. This interchange includes the idea of the *figurant*, which J.O.I. uses to describe himself. Originally a French term for background ballet dancers, it has been applied to actors on stage and, later, in movies and television. Like the intubated Gately and the wraith, these figurants are said to have no voice in the performances of sitcoms, and *Cheers*, the 1980s television show set in a Boston bar, is the example given. Countless bar patrons talk and emote in its scenes but are never heard. Gately equates these people to something like "human furniture," "*figurants* the wraith says they're called" (835). The ghost of Incandenza admits that "he personally spent the vast bulk of his own former animate life as pretty much a figurant, furniture to the periphery of the very eyes closest to him." The pain-addled Gately begins to confuse the two terms *wraith* and *figurant*: "He wonders what something as brief as a car-horn-honk sounds like to a figurant that has to sit still for three weeks to be seen. Wraith, not figurant, Gately meant, he corrects himself" (837). If Gately is not moved by the plight of the figurant/wraith, he will not get involved with the wraith's son and will not join him in the effort to recover the master copy of *Infinite Jest*. Though probably unsuccessful given the already wide distribution of the copies of the film, we know that Hal in the Year of Glad at the beginning of the novel remembers "John N. R. Wayne … standing watch in a mask as Donald Gately and I dig up my father's head" (17–8). This interaction is fundamental in linking the two main protagonists of the novel through the ghost of Incandenza and to connecting the images of the final pages of *IJ* back to the opening sequence.

The ghostwords and the idea of a *figurant* are essential to a reading of *Infinite Jest* as a ghost story as Frye and other critics often do with *Hamlet*. They are one of the important ways that both DFW and J.O.I. communicate some of the most essential connections of this story through its *Hamlet*-content. Moreover, these ideas are instrumental in convincing Gately to get a message to Himself's son, Hal.

Infinite Jest and *Hamlet* are connected not only directly through the paradigms of the text of Shakespeare's *Hamlet*, but also by looking at important literary criticisms of *Hamlet* like that of Roland Mushat Frye in *The Renaissance* Hamlet (1984), which Wallace might have encountered. Mourning, incest, and the importance of the ghost within the text are just three of the issues Frye elucidates that one can directly connect to *IJ* through *Hamlet*; others are the skull metaphor, the "court," and the idea of the grave. Whether he read Frye's thought-provoking look at how Shakespeare's contemporary audience may have viewed *Hamlet* or not, Wallace has filled his novel with many less-than-obvious connections to *Hamlet*, which will continue to provide fruitful sources of intertextual research for me and others for years to come.

Works Cited

Alexander, Nigel. *Poison, Play, and Duel: a Study in* Hamlet. U of Nebraska P, 1971.

Frye, Roland Mushat. *The Renaissance* Hamlet*: Issues and Responses in 1600*. Princeton UP, 1984.

Goodwin, Jonathon. "Wallace's *Infinite Jest*." *Explicator*, vol. 61, no. 2, Winter 2003, 122–25.

Shakespeare, William. *The Tragedy of Hamlet, Prince of Denmark. The Norton Shakespeare: Based on the Oxford Edition*. W.W. Norton and Co., 1997.

Skeat, James William, Rev. "Fourteenth Address of the President, to the Philological Society, Delivered at the Anniversary Meeting, Friday 21 May 1886." 21 May 1886. *Wiley Online Library*, Wiley, Mar. 2008, onlinelibrary.wiley.com/doi/10.1111/j.1467-968X.1887.tb00113.x/abstract. Accessed 13 Aug. 2016.

Wallace, David Foster. *Infinite Jest*. Little, Brown and Company, 1996.

Infinite Jest, Postmodernism, and Irony: A Brief Guide to Happiness in Our Contemporary Age
Alexander C. Ruhsenberger

As far back as I can remember, I wanted to be a postmodernist. When I began my undergraduate degree, postmodernism was the hip thing to study. My entry level writing class, taught by a recent MA graduate, scrutinized not just traditional English classroom fare but SkyMall ads, hipster philosophy, and pulp phenomena in U.S. culture. But it wasn't just the young MA graduates: older professors, too, espoused the prose of Pynchon and DeLillo—after all, these authors saw the world "the way it is," impartial to any imposed meaning. My professors grew up with postmodernism, and I grew up with postmodernism, too. It seems the movement, idea, and word itself, now spans three generations if not four generations. Even in the digital age, it retains its position as the dominant literary and cultural force. Postmodernism towers, imperturbable, as a kind of bookend, and the last of the literary ages. It seems symbolic of the end of time. For a millennial like myself, this is fascinating, because I was born in 1991, at the end of time. In 2009—Wallace's Year of Glad—I graduated high school. And now here I am—applying to doctoral programs, and grappling with the tangled tendrils of postmodernism in the twenty-first century. While sometimes it feels as if my academic ancestors invented postmodernism to suppress any new idea, definition, and concept, I've come to understand a few ideas of importance in my time.

I first came to Wallace through his famous "This is Water" speech.[1] There, each of his fears, his thoughts, his concerns and idiosyncratic mannerisms seemed to indicate a wealth of lifetime wisdom earned, and in one enlightening deliverance, I saw him as the pre-eminent thinker and orator of his time. Shortly afterward, I bought *Infinite Jest*.[2] The novel was anything but like his speech. Wallace demands much from his readers, and he doesn't always make it clear why or even *if* follow-thru and completion is worth it. So for a time I put *Infinite Jest* on hold and read some of his nonfiction work, particularly his

---

1 David Foster Wallace, *This is Water*, (Little, Brown and Company, 2009).
2 Wallace, *Infinite Jest*, (Bay Back Books, 2006).

article "E Unibus Pluram: Television and U.S. Fiction."[3] In that article, Wallace did something for postmodernism and postmodern culture that I hadn't quite considered: he designated irony as the attitude representing our current literary movement. He took Soren Kierkegaard's existential irony—irony that has to do with how you live your life, and how sincerely you treat your existence on this Earth (rather than say simply linguistic irony)—and attached it to postmodernism.[4] In other words, Wallace gave postmodernity an attitude—a look, a style, and a pose—a character, a face, and a quintessential smirk. Not that it didn't already have these features before; Wallace just happened to point them out in a single essayistic stride: on the TV. He pulled back the postmodern skin; he made it look human and fallible in the grand scheme of the world. At the same time, he shined a light on its philosophical meanderings and masks. With guts and ease Wallace anthropomorphized something that shouldn't have been anthropomorphized. This gesture liberated me from a prison of thought. The moment was tremendously exciting—like a brand new universe of ideas was now unfolding before me. Wallace was pulling apart some of my professor's most revered novelists, stating, "The novels of Pynchon and DeLillo revolve metaphorically off the concept of interference: the more connections, the more chaos, and the harder it is to cull meaning from the seas of signal."[5] He took the intricacies of this chaos, this TV culture and existential irony, and tied it altogether, labeling culture with character, writing:

> Irony in postwar art and culture started out the same way youthful rebellion did. It was difficult and painful, and productive—a grim diagnosis of a long-denied disease. The assumptions *behind* early postmodern irony, on the other hand, were still frankly idealistic: it was assumed that etiology and diagnosis pointed toward cure, that a revelation of imprisonment led to freedom.[6]

In the end, his contemporaries regarded Wallace as a kind of cultural rockstar—after all, he put the ironic face on postmodernity. He called the movement for what it was and is, straight out, with little reservation. He denounced the awareness of postmodern irony as a hopeless self-consciousness fed-up with itself. He took the idea of existential irony—this idea coming all the way from Kierkegaard about the inability for an individual to be free if he

---

3 Wallace, "E Unibus Pluram: Television and U.S. Fiction," in *A Supposedly Fun Thing I'll Never do Again,* (Back Bay Books, 1998).
4 Allard Den Dulk, "Beyond Endless 'Aesthetic' Irony: A Comparison of the Irony Critique of Soren Kierkegaard and David Foster Wallace's *Infinite Jest,*" *Studies in the Novel,* 44 no. 3 (2012).
5 Wallace, "E Unibus Pluram," 73.
6 Ibid., 66-67.

has no real connection with his world—and tied it right into the now: with the user surfing channels, empty, lonely, lost in a sea of culture, jaded, ironic, anhedonic, catatonic, traveling at light speed with their mere finger tips, and yet going nowhere. The essay read darkly, brutal even. It was a diagnosis of a culture that's chief, most earnest signature was its resistance to diagnosis, which believed that embracing chaos with self-awareness was the most intelligent, whole, fulfilled, and even just plain old happy thing one could pursue…

It was exciting because postmodernism is a bizarre post-World War II phenomenon we've all had to contend with in some fashion. Fredric Jameson identified the postmodern as a kind of "schizophrenic" aesthetic and world view: that the world we know has a massive chaotic bent, and the relationships between objects, ideas, fashions, events, moments, are tentative and coincidental at best.[7] And like the schizophrenic viewer himself, these relationship are also random in their underlying structure. Jameson argued that a postmodern culture, taken to its most extreme extent, would embrace this kind of schizophrenic treatment of sign and signifier.[8] And although Wallace never talked too explicitly about sign and signifier, the breakdown of the connection between the two—between the message and its meaning—is another way of expressing Wallace's concerns about culture. The problem is postmodernism supposes that the sign is irreparably damaged, and that it will never perfectly, or even imperfectly, lead to the signifier. This is a hard concept to grasp if you don't imagine it on every possible level. Every connection you can make, every mental analogy, every memory or image you think to be pure; every word you say; every organization you are a part of is somehow diluted and open to a false interpretation. What is sent on one end is tampered with on the other. The concept betrays a fascination with paranoia: *the structure of everything is irrevocably tainted and corrupt.* Welcome to the TV age, the internet age, where anything and anyone can be ironized. Wallace, a new age traditionalist raised on TV, fought hard against this. He called it irony. He believed that this mode of thought lead to a society of individuals who believe in chaos; in nothing; in addiction; in pleasure alone: hedonistic, nihilistic, catatonic, trapped on the inside, lonely in a crowd of others, and obsessed with the image of the culture in the here and now.

All of this, of course, exists mostly in the imagination. We don't live like this on a day-to-day basis—our society could not function in complete

---

7 Fredric Jameson, *Postmodernism or, The Cultural Logic of Late Capitalism* (Duke UP, 1991), 26.
8 Ibid., 27-29.

postmodernity. Parts of it may manifest these ideas, but they are constantly kept in balance with ideas of structure, order, semblance and harmony among things. The most pure form of postmodernism is what Wallace details as post-postmodernism, or the catatonic, as written about by Hal in his essay in *Infinite Jest*.[9] In this idea, the self-awareness afforded by the chaos of sign and signifier becomes a kind of religion, or a way to live one's life by said chaos. So in the novel *Infinite Jest*, Wallace imagined an apocalyptic scenario: he foresaw a society living in total postmodernity—a society that reckoned with the truly, utterly ironic.

The opening sequence of *Infinite Jest* reflects these ideas and fears. It's a scene in the Year of Glad, when Hal is attempting to get into Arizona State University. In the university's admissions office, two sets of adults argue, deliberate, and communicate on behalf of Hal. For the first seven pages of the novel, Hal can't get in a word. Eventually he is implored to speak for himself. Needless to say, his attempt at connection does not go well. He states that he is "not just a boy who plays tennis. I have an intricate history. Experiences and feelings. I'm complex."[10] Hal aptly ends this thought with: "I am not what you see and hear."[11] But these words are not heard by the characters sitting across from him: the administrators have Hal restrained and taken out on stretcher, for all they can hear is the most hideous of noises and the wildest of facial and bodily expressions. "What's wrong?" one dean asks in panic. Hal says, "Nothing is wrong." But the director is yelling, "Sweet mother of Christ," and someone else is calling for an ambulance.[12] Hal is then, of course, shuttled off, catatonic, as humorously referenced in one of this seventh grade essays—as he is now seemingly the post-postmodern hero.[13] So postmodern, in fact, that he is entirely unable to communicate.

This is a fascinating sequence, because Wallace presents us with a culture wherein the adults (the bastions and high minds of culture, arts, and the sciences) are not only unsympathetic, but also incapable of moving beyond their own cultural moment. As Hal is being hauled off to E.R., one dean says, "… [you] think you could pass off a damaged applicant, fabricate credentials and shunt him through a kangaroo-interview and inject him into all the rigors of college life?"[14] The dean says this, legitimately, as if all that

---

9 Wallace, *Infinite Jest*, 142.
10 Ibid., 11.
11 Ibid., 13.
12 Ibid., 12.
13 Ibid., 142.
14 Ibid., 15.

matters at this point is academic prestige. It's indicative of Wallace's critique of postmodernism and irony, in that these characters live in an age where a young, sensitive individual can become trapped on the inside because all his culture can "see" of him is his exterior—a surface level diagnosis. So the world of *Infinite Jest* is precisely unliterary, and its people cannot see the genius of culture because they can only see reality for its face-value. They, like the deans, see with a surface culture's schizophrenia: a pile of idle signs with no internal spirit or essence. Or, said more precisely, they are a world of people without structure. Perhaps this explains why so many of the character are addicts, susceptible to drugs, entertainment, or The Entertainment in Wallace's imagination. They are ironic in that they do not believe in anything. In Hal's case, I believe he eventually becomes something more than this: that he pulls out of his irony. But then, in the Year of Glad, his revelation doesn't matter to the world because the world can't hear him anymore. This might explain why Hal's father's creation—the film "Infinite Jest"—is so destructive; why many of the novels characters feel an indescribable horror; why Joelle hides behind a vail; and why no other American character, as Marathe and Steeply denote, are truly free, despite knowing and worshiping the word freedom.[15]

Of course, these are all old ideas—ideas that Wallace illuminated in his "This is Water" speech, and ideas that Wallace believed culture could live by and has lived by: that in the end, real, individual choice can overcome default thinking, permitting a freedom of choice, as opposed to only a freedom to be ironic toward something.

But despite these ideas, postmodernism and irony fascinate me still. This fascination has something to do with a quote from *Either/Or* by Kierkegaard:
> There is a wretched unbelief abroad which seems to contain much healing power. It deems such [connections] accidental, and sees in it only a lucky conjunction of the different forces in the game of life. It thinks it an accident that the lovers win one another, accidental that they love one another; there were a hundred other women with whom the hero might have been equally happy [with] …[16]

The "wretched unbelief" could be considered the precursor to Wallace's brand of irony. This belief demonstrates that this ironic problem in *Infinite Jest* is far older than postmodernism or post-postmodernism; in many ways, it appears in the novel as a description of anhedonia, in which the

---

15 Ibid., 320.
16 Soren Kierkegaard, *Either/or: Volume I*, trans. David F. Swenson and Lillian Marvin Swenson (Princeton UP, 1971), 45.

anhedonic individuals hollow out all meaning and live empty lives.[17] Wallace even borrows the term "*Weltschmerz*," with its meaning "world-weariness," in which educated individuals linger on the dead obsessions of what it is cool and hip and unsentimental and self-aware, but are unable to meaningfully engage in a way that makes them feel whole—sort of like post-postmodernity.[18] Taken in whole, Wallace's irony seems notably similar to the kind of ironic unbelief that Kierkegaard talks about in his passage from *Either/Or*. As such, Wallace's focal issue affects much more than his stand-in for a millennial, Hal, but the whole millennial generation as well; that generation which already has subscribed to the intercommunication of all human beings through fibre optic lines, and a generation subscribed to streaming far away pulses replicating human behavior, and the infinite abundance of information, science, and diagnosis; a generation who thinks love is a happy accident; whose postmodern outlook is so extreme, whose grasp of psychology and science is so entrenched, that they've (in part) lost the ability to see what lacks coincidence. Nothing is *meant* to be, in the human world. Like the postmodern dystopic fantasy in *Infinite Jest*, and like the dean who understands his academy and only his academy, most of the world becomes a giant collision of signals bouncing off each other, and your small signal bubble is the only one that matters. In short: the future world is material, Hal is diagnosable, and pleasure and addiction define freedom in *Infinite Jest's* America.

Perhaps what Wallace laments, which manifests itself as a film than can incapacitate any human being, a plague like "world-weariness," an indefinable horror, an AA program, a president who is catatonic, and a young man who can speak well but has to learn how to communicate, is indicative of a bizarre new-age world view that has been growing for the last two-hundred years in the Western world (possibly longer) that has come to mean the end of humanity's spiritualism. Call it postmodernism, call it irony, call it what you like, but Wallace and many knew it was, just, like…there. I don't mean spiritualism in the religious sense; I mean it in the greater implication that culture itself is no longer belief-worthy, which is again said best by Kierkegaard: as belief in "unbelief." But what literature has always taught me—and what in many ways *Infinite Jest* teaches me—is that the world is a giant interconnected web of patterns, meanings, and contexts. I can see this clearly, intuitively, but it is often hard to describe with mere words. It has to do with the fact (and feeling too) that we human beings are all pattern makers—we are all born with this gift: to make complex and sophisticated patterns of our world and to see the interconnectedness of even our tiny existence. To by extent assert our

---

17 Wallace, *Infinite Jest*, 693.
18 Ibid., 694.

vision, our individuality, and an ability to make something of the universe and to share and respect others visions around us. To see how the world of all things, however complex, is one organism, breathing and flexing, and made up the individuality of all of us simultaneously. It is this ability—to make order out of chaos—that makes us human. In *Return of the Jedi*,[19] when Luke Skywalker cuts off Darth Vader's hand during their final confrontation, he takes a moment to look at his own hand, which his father cut off in a previous duel. Here, Luke sees a vital connection, a human connection, in the universe out there in the stars. In one climactic moment, he realizes how small his vengeance and wrath really are. At the end of *When Harry met Sally...*, Harry runs toward Sally on New Year's Eve to tell her his romantic epiphany: "When you realize you want to spend the rest of your life with someone, you want the rest of your life to start right now."[20] In *Hamlet* the titular character questions the very fabric of life itself, poised on the edge of sanity, with "To be or not to be—that is the question," and for "When we have shuffled off this mortal coil,/must give us pause. There's the respect/That makes calamity of so long life."[21] And Wallace's own Hal breaks from a family tradition of tennis, begins to unwind, and becomes sincere for something, anything, at precisely the moment his culture can no longer hear or see him. All these instances and more show humanity coming to sense with the story. This tangibly production of A Why, the reasoning of actions and choices, and the meaning or pattern of life and the universe at large, are what a friend and I have coined "thematic exposition." From what I can tell, this is one of the most critical and pertinent parts of literature and art. For example: when I say that I study literature, I mean that I study thematic exposition—not just entertainment, or consumption, or piles of endless old dusty novels—but patterns, attempts at patterns, and what those patterns mean in the fabric of the great human cycle of things. So what shocks me is the idea of a generation that can no longer see the world in this literary light. A generation which would lack individuals who could see beyond, and individuals not capable of seeing the literary connections and interconnectedness of all things. Rather, this generation sees merely the literal, the surface, the what-is-there-in-front-of-me-now. This is the "wretched unbelief" that Kierkegaard talks about, in which love is an accident, even when this generation could imagine love to be

---

19 *Star Wars: Episode VI - Return of the Jedi*, directed by Richard Marquand (1983; Twentieth Century Fox Home Entertainment, 2004), DVD.
20 *When Harry Met Sally...*, directed by Rob Reiner (1989; Twentieth Century Fox Home Entertainment, 2011), DVD.
21 William Shakespeare,"To be, or not to be, that is the question" from *Hamlet*, from *Poetry Foundation*, n.d., July 18, 2016. https://www.poetryfoundation.org/poems-and-poets.

something more if they choose. They could choose a different meaning, but they won't: they will swipe left for dislike and swipe right for like. The shrewd post-postmodernism blinds us—assuming that even in a world where we can make any connection we want or choose, that life is nothing but an infinite cloud of beeping lights and signals—incommunicable, unworthy of pattern, belief, or greater meaning other than to justify its own chaos. We would take the most beautiful of gifts, phenomenological existence, a miracle, and call it an accident: nothing more than a marketplace of breeding. What funny creatures we are.

At the end of Wallace's "E Unibus Pluram" essay, he half-heartedly supposes that a future generation will come about who will risk a new kind of dullness—a banal, or overwrought sentiment—to counter a postmodern culture that is ironic to no real end.[22] Wallace puts this forth as a kind of final thought, and I don't think, with sincerity, that he would have left it that way today. It seems the future problem, as even *Infinite Jest* shows us, is vastly more complex. Thinking with naivety and innocence does not redeem us from what postmodernism gave us when it showed us the potential chaos of the world. Even old postmodernism opened up or tried to open up the idea of the complexity of the world around us, and the inability for the sign to match its meaning, and its vast implications; at least we got a sense of the scope of things. But I think the naiveness of the so called post-postmodernity is far too dangerous—to go about teaching our children that life defaults to the unstructured and the chaotic, to which the only solace is, "Why bother figuring it out?" before resting easy. Conversely, sincerity with naivety only presents us with a totalitarian ideology that of which history has taught us is equally destructive if not more so. But certainly a world where there is only "…a lucky conjunction of the different forces in the game of life," is also troubling and unimaginative. And so it requires a great deal more skill and knowledge to teach those "to see a world in a grain of sand/and a Heaven in a wild flower."[23] I think this kind of challenge for a generation coming after irony, after postmodernism, after whatever it is that needs to come after the after, is a challenge to really open their eyes. This is about seeing a world full of dense, nuanced, intricate, and meaningful connections, and teaching this perspective is far more difficult than teaching irony, or sincerity, or passive worship. When I teach my students, I first and foremost teach them to make as many connections as possible, and to explain and understand why they made such connections, rather than merely teaching them to be postmodernists.

---

22 Wallace, "E Unibus Pluram," 81-82.
23 William Blake, "Auguries of Innocence," from *Poetry Foundation,* n.d., July 18, 2016. http://www.poetryfoundation.org/poems-and-poets/poems/detail/43650#poem.

This is a revelation that is earned, even in our fast and loose, supposedly globalized twenty-first century.

But it occurs to me that these problems—of postmodernism, post-postmodernism perhaps, irony, sincerity, and the themes by which we construct our lives—are what make *Infinite Jest* so important as a millennial novel. And make no mistake about that: *Infinite Jest* is a millennial novel dealing with millennial issues and with the millennial generation (particularly Hal) and the overload of information and potential anhedonic abstracting of humanity that would come to define this strange new age. And the reason *Infinite Jest* resonates with so many millennials is that Wallace, by accident or intention, created a world not so far unlike the one this current generation is approaching; he created a world where individuals see nothing more than lucky conjunctions, where individuals are not taught how to worship or what to worship, or even if they should worship. It is a world where life has lost its meaning and semblance of sincerity to the throes of an attitude: irony. Wallace's response is also appealing to me, as a millennial who feels as if his world isn't just falling apart (as I am sure every generation has felt the apocalyptic in some fashion or another), but that something is missing: a literary and thematic sight. Because the faster the world develops, the more information pulses through the highways of fibre optic lines and networks, and the more I feel that there may not be time to slow down and look closer and "pay attention," as Wallace would say. And for that reason, the novel is unfettered, dark, but also slow and refreshing even.

One of the most frightening parts of the novel is Wallace's rhetoric using President Jonny Gentle, which has an uneasy comparison to current politics wrapped up not only in image, but in a perverse kind of isolationism, insularism, and anhedonia, best embodied by Gentle's abuse of Canada and Mexico, and dissolution of NATO.[24] Gentle, as Wallace teases, "...swears he'll find us some cohesion-renewing Other. And then make tough choices."[25] He is a president who first and foremost, like the deans at Arizona State, is speaking to a bubbled generation—a generation who have insulated their roles, their humanity, and their ideas—who ultimately fail to connect. I guess the bitter pill to swallow is that despite advancements in entertainment technology and abilities and ways to communicate, these advances only further people's vain and self-reflective desires, so that we may be the center of our own tiny worlds. Even if we have no "Other," we need to make one. Wallace seems to suggest that despite access to a great world of entertainment and information

---

24 Wallace, *Infinite Jest*, 385-86.
25 Ibid., 384.

and knowledge on the human, we are still afraid of what is outside of us, what is "Other." And the default cynicism and irony from postmodernism is a default because the single-entendre values seem inane, and impossible to surmount in their gooey simplistic state.

Perhaps that is the fascination with a character like Mario, a single-entendre, faith-filled individual in a world of irony. I think this also explains the millennial Hal, who is in Wallace's terms is: "…empty but not dumb, [but] theorizes privately that what passes for hip cynical transcendence of sentiment is really some kind of fear of being really human…"[26] Thinking about Hal now, in 2016, with a president Gentle on the potential horizon, I am a little frightened by a rising insularism and inability to see a greater human perspective in our world. I think it's a key problem because it's very tempting to be like Hal: to lose faith in humanity; to embrace the new politics of cutting yourself off from the rest of the world; to be frightened by the human. It's not like I am some extreme neoliberalist who seeks to control everything under one banner; but at the same time, I really do want to have a kind of master faith in humanity. I, like Wallace, lament Hal's state. I have to admit, at the end of a day, a little weary, that my heart wants to believe the dumb principle of some lost hippie age, in which I ask: can the world be one? Can we all unite under the banner of human? Perhaps this simplistic, overly sincere, singular principle is the most valuable concept of all: that the true challenge is to see all that sincerity and earnestness and hope, as well as all that despair, and to take it seriously, even beneath all the irony, double meanings, and endless confusion of our everyday lives, there's a united idea of humanity worth believing in.

---

26 Ibid, 694.

David Foster Wallace, Heidegger, and Postmodern Irony
Danny Sheaf

This paper draws on Martin Heidegger's hermeneutic phenomenology to consider David Foster Wallace's negotiation of the problem of postmodern irony. I will contend that Wallace's critique is concerned with postmodern irony as a cultural force which has shaped our understanding of ourselves. For Wallace, postmodern irony presupposes perpetual self-reflection, leading to self-alienation. An attitude becomes ironic when the self (supposedly) divides into parts: one that is unreflective, and one that reflectively observes that other part. This reflective process is infinite; every point of view becomes the object of another point of view. Following Wallace's account, I argue that the postmodern ironist is trapped in this unending process of self-reflection whereby others and the meaningful world are "lost." Wallace's characters in *Infinite Jest* play out the paradox of living within a cultural climate defined by postmodern irony where their actions are mediated by a self-reflective distancing which is, ultimately, an impossible position based on a cultural-theoretical presupposition which we take to be true. With Heidegger, I argue that the postmodern ironist's "inward" turn is based on the mistaken assumption that human "lived-experience" is an object which can be isolated from the "outside" world. Heidegger's phenomenological project, and in particular his concept of *authenticity*, offers a response to postmodern irony which allows us to take into account others, the world, and our own participation in it.

Wallace's theory of postmodernism, as developed in "E Unibus Pluram," marks postmodernism as both a literary movement and a cultural condition.[1] Following this argument, I will discuss postmodernism as a particular theoretical approach to language which has come to define contemporary culture rather than give an account of any one thinker. Postmodernism, in this

---

1 Wallace, David Foster. "E Unibus Pluram: Television and U.S. Fiction." *Review of Contemporary Fiction*. 13.2. 1993: 151–194.

sense, is a style of thought which is critical of the "realist" assumption that language can offer a neutral representation of reality.

This critique of postmodernism and postmodern irony does have a basis in the field of Wallace scholarship. Following the initial insights of Marshall Boswell, there is a burgeoning field which seeks to think through the proposed "solipsism" of postmodern irony. However, this concept has generally been taken to be an issue specific to communication rather than a broader problem concerning our thinking about "self" and "world".[2] Wallace points to Wittgenstein's *Philosophical Investigations* as an initial influence for this cultural turn toward the ironist. That is, if we take language to be our entire existence it opens up the possibility of taking our existence as an "object" of investigation. Much of Wallace's oeuvre can, I suggest, be read as an attempt to write against the "postmodern trap" which reduces meaning and lived-experience to language which we could take as a static object of reflection and which, through an ironic attitude, we could distance ourselves from. I suggest that this issue can be re-framed by moving away from a linguistic analysis of irony and considering a phenomenological approach. I will outline such an approach below.

The critique of irony outlined in Wallace's fiction initially stems from a theoretical linguistic problem which Wallace suggests has seeped into cultural understanding. That is, it has come to affect the self-understanding of the contemporary individual within the present culture. Wallace argued, from the very beginning of his career, that the "trap" of postmodern irony was a direct follow-on from the insights of Wittgenstein. In an early interview Wallace states that,

> This was Wittgenstein's double bind: you can either treat language as an infinitely small dense dot, or you let it become the world.... The latter seems more promising. If the world is itself a linguistic construct, there's nothing 'outside' language.... [This] leads right to the postmodern, post-structural dilemma of having to deny yourself an existence independent of language.[3]

Wallace, drawing from Wittgenstein's critique of ostensive teaching and a private language, suggests that the postmodern "trap" stems from thinking that takes language to *be* our "reality."[4] The problem which he identifies, then,

---

2 Boswell, Marshall. *Understanding David Foster Wallace*. U of South Carolina, 2003.
3 McCaffery, Larry. "An Interview with David Foster Wallace." *Review of Contemporary Fiction*. 13 (2), 1993: 127–150.
4 See: Wittgenstein, Ludwig. *Philosophical Investigations*. Farmington Hills, MI, United States: Cengage Gale, 1973.

is that we have no "referent" which language can be compared to. Hence, we reach the postmodern notion that truth is a linguistic construct. Language, then, is not a neutral medium which points to a referent "in the world." Wallace seems to suggest that the recognition of this issue has subsequently provided the platform for the phenomenon of "postmodern irony." This form of irony was initially employed as a critical device in postmodern fiction. The problem, for Wallace, stems from its subsequent adoption into mainstream media. Instead of being a critique, it has become "reality" itself.

For Wallace, "televisual culture" has adopted irony, which was once a means for rebellion against mass culture, by transforming irony into a cultural norm.[5] Wallace suggests that irony has become the discourse of the postmodern culture. Social life, informed by television, has become steeped in irony. In 1993 Wallace notes: "the fact is that for at least ten years now, television has been ingeniously absorbing, homogenizing, and re-representing the very same cynical postmodern aesthetic that was once the best alternative to the appeal of low, over-easy, mass-marketed narrative."[6]

Wallace alleges that television has a precarious capacity to shape the ways in which a culture sees itself. What is new to television's methods, Wallace argues, is that it has adopted and transformed the techniques from postmodern literature, once used to critique the present, namely, those of postmodern irony, into its own method, to affirm its own practices.[7] Advertisements, in an effort to keep the viewer watching, have utilised the technique of postmodern self-referentiality, supposedly undermining advertising's own practice by affirming its own manipulative intentions. That is, advertising uses irony to expose *and* disguise its own agenda, thereby "insulating" itself from the criticism that would come from the viewer. Postmodern *fiction* initially used this form of irony to expose and question the realist assumption that there was something like a reality "behind" language. The problem Wallace identifies is that, as a cultural attitude, postmodern irony operates to separate ourselves from our lived-experience through constant self-reflection.

This attitude finds philosophical expression in Richard Rorty, an American theorist writing around the same time as Wallace. Rorty, I argue, represents the above mentioned connection between language, irony and self-reflection.

---

5 Wallace, writing in the early 90's, focusses exclusively on television. While it is questionable whether we still live in an age of "televisual culture," I suggest that new mediums such as internet social media only extend the ironic attitude as I outline it here.

6 Ibid., 45.

7 Ibid., 50-53.

Sheaf

Following Wittgenstein, Rorty starts from the assumption that truth and knowledge are a social construct born out of any given community's "linguistic practices". That is, we do not have a concept of something because we have noticed it in sense perception but we come to notice it because we have the concept of it; even simple perception requires other knowledge. For Rorty, the other knowledge which is required is given to us by our participation in our shared "linguistic community." As Rorty puts it, "there is no such thing as justification which is not a relation between propositions."[8] We do not speak of meanings which exist outside of language. All beliefs and concepts are purely linguistic.

Following this assumption, any justification would be circular because an attempt to rationalise one's view would already be based on the language game which the individual has inherited. All justifications for our vocabulary would simply point to other words within the language game without any recourse to a non-contingent foundation. Therefore, any claims articulated within one's linguistic tradition cannot be justified at all. On this position, there cannot be some non-contingent foundation. An awareness of this groundlessness opens up the possibility of "irony."[9]

According to Rorty, the opposite of irony is common sense, "for that is the watchword of those who unselfconsciously describe everything important in terms of the final vocabulary to which they and those around them are habituated."[10] "Non-intellectuals," as Rorty calls them, simply accept common sense and do not ask questions about the foundation of that which they take to be true. "Non-intellectuals" would simply accept the immediacy of their cultural discourse. For Rorty, then, the task of the ironist is to escape from inherited vocabularies by "re-describing" oneself. In a fight against this notion of "common sense," Rorty understands freedom in terms of self-creation or the achievement of a kind of radical individualism. As I will discuss below, I argue that one simply cannot "construct" one's own mind so as to leave the influence of the contingent world completely. Rorty's postmodern irony is not directed against specific claims that are part of inherited meaning but against the notion of foundational meaning itself.

This is the negative tendency of postmodern irony which Wallace identifies; it destroys all the foundations from which one can claim meaning. Again, this is the case for Rorty, because "meaning" is purely linguistic, embedded in one's

---

8 Rorty, Richard. *Philosophy and the Mirror of Nature*. Princeton UP, 1979, 183.
9 Rorty, Richard. *Contingency, Irony and Solidarity*. Cambridge UP, 1989, 73.
10 Ibid., 73.

contingent language. In Rortian irony, I argue, the ironist's detachment from her own "world-view" simply generates another point of view, so that whatever the ironist seeks to express is already undercut by her position as a part of a purely contingent linguistic community. This is the apparent contradiction of postmodern irony; the purposed cultural and historical contingency of any claim is not overcome by irony; the ironist cannot think from a place which is not a part of any historical context. As Claire Colebrook expresses it, "this unintended contradiction is manifestly exploited in much postmodern ironic literature."[11] This literature attempts to use irony to destabilise its own contingent position and hence to show its contingency. Following this attempt to show the contingency of language, Colebrook claims that postmodern irony is a movement that "'quotes,' 'mentions' or repeats styles, without any sense of a proper or privileged style, and with a sense that one set of concepts is no more 'proper' or grounded than another."[12] The postmodern ironist undercuts their own position, effectively saying nothing at all. Importantly, as I already noted, Wallace argues that this theme has not been confined to literature but has been appropriated by advertising and, subsequently, has come to shape our modern self-understanding.

The Rortian ironist is, I argue, endlessly self-reflective. The ironist must perform the role of the unreflective "non-intellectual" in public; however, this point of view is then "observed" by the ironist in private. Yet, this point of view is still bound to the contingencies of language; hence a further reflection and separation from language is required and so on to infinity. Each point of view would be caught in an infinite regress of self-reflection all based on the original *performance* of the "public self." Irony, Paul de Man explains, "engenders a temporal sequence of acts of consciousness which is endless. Irony is not temporary but repetitive, the recurrence of a self-escalating act of consciousness."[13] De Man defines this reflective process as infinite; every point of view becomes immediately the object of another point of view. Likewise, I suggest, the ironist does not in fact attain the liberation which Rorty attributes to the position. The ironist, in effect, becomes nothing but a self-reflective performer. Wallace compares this act of infinite self-reflection to drug addiction. He states that "99% of compulsive thinkers' thinking is about themselves…most Substance-addicted people are also addicted to thinking, meaning they have a compulsive and unhealthy relationship with

---

11 Colebrook, Claire. *Irony*. Routledge, 2004, 64.
12 Colebrook, Claire. *Irony in the Work of Philosophy*. U of Nebraska P, 2002. 227.
13 De Man. Paul. *Blindness and Insight: Essays in the Rhetoric of Contemporary Criticism*. Methuen, 1983, 220.

their own thinking."[14] This is the cultural issue which, I argue, Wallace is attempting to think through in his fiction.

Wallace exposes the infinite regress of self-reflective irony through various characters who seemingly divide into separate states of reflection where they observe themselves observing. We can see, in the case of *Infinite Jest*, that the narrator, Hal Incandenza, has succumbed to this ironic attitude where he reflects on his own reflection:

> Hal wonders, not for the first time, whether he might deep down be a snob about collar-color issues…then whether the fact that he's capable of wondering whether he's a snob attenuates the possibility that he's really a snob.[15]

Hal's reflection, of course, only sends him into a spiraling self-examination further divorced from the original question of class-consciousness, leading him into "analysis paralysis." The ironic attitude amounts to a total rejection of meaning. Any significance tied to the original question is lost to recursive self-reflection. For Wallace, postmodern irony necessarily leads to a kind of radical subjectivism. Hal is representative of what I refer to as the ironist. *Infinite Jest* begins with the scene as narrated by Hal, which is, arguably, the chronological conclusion of the story.

> I am seated in an office, surrounded by heads and bodies. My posture is consciously congruent to the shape of my hard chair.… I believe I appear neutral, maybe even pleasant, though I've been coached to err on the side of neutrality.[16]

Hal's experience is presented as that of a subject observing objects "outside" of himself. He also describes himself and his appearance as something distant to his own "experience." Hal is, in a sense, "outside" of himself. In the novel, his subjectivism is taken to the extreme conclusion whereby he literally cannot interact with the world at all. Hal can neither move nor speak in a way that appears remotely "human" to the other people in the room. His attempts at interaction are described as "subanimalistic" noises and gestures. Hal's predicament in this first scene can be read as a *reductio ad absurdum* of Rorty's ironist; for the radical individualism of the "re-described" ironist seemingly separates one from others and from oneself. Beyond this, from the beginning, Wallace exposes the reader to the horrors of solipsism showing how the ironist achieves a theoretical separation from their own lived-experience.

The solipsism and emptiness of the postmodern/linguistic trap is personified through the characters Hal Incandenza and Joelle Van Dyne. Hal is described

---

14 Wallace, David Foster. *Infinite Jest*. Abacus, 1997, 380.

15 Ibid., 380.

16 Ibid., 1.

as a linguistic genius. His analytic aptitude only leads him to complete solipsism as outlined above. Wallace also shows the impossibility of this position, leading Hal to a spiralling self-awareness. Similarly, Joelle cannot experience anything as meaningful or significant since any possible striving for meaning is destroyed by her theoretical linguistic analysis. This serves to distance her from actually "living through" and understanding the meaning of the *Alcoholics Anonymous* phrases which saved one narrator, Don Gately, from a life of drugs and crime:

> [She] says that she's finding it especially hard to take when these earnest ravaged folks at the lectern say they're 'Here But For the Grace of God'…when Gately nods hard and starts to interject about the 'God' in the slogan being just shorthand for a 'Higher Power'…. Joelle cuts off his interjection and says that…'But For the Grace of God' is a subjunctive, a counterfactual, she says, and can make sense only when introducing a conditional clause…. 'I'm here But For the Grace of God' is, she says, literally senseless, and regardless of whether she hears it or not it's meaningless.[17]

Joelle's astute analysis of the AA slogan may be correct, although the meaning of the phrase is, for Gately, something separate from the literal linguistic expression. Wallace continually reminds the reader that these slogans must be *lived through*. As I will discuss with reference to Heidegger, propositional language, as static, is separate from lived-experience which cannot be made objective and cannot be separate from us who live it. What is ignored by Joelle is the actual meaning as it is understood by the speaker and the "AA" audience alike. If we reduce meaning to propositional language we lose something fundamental to our lived-experience; we objectify and separate ourselves from this experience. As Wallace shows through his fiction, the individual who understands their lived-experience as an object separate from themselves are subject to what Wallace calls "anhedonia." As we see in the character of Kate Gompert, the "anhedonic" loses something fundamental to being a human being.

> Kate Gompert's always thought of this anhedonic state as a kind of radical abstracting of everything, a hollowing out of stuff that used to have affective content…. The anhedonic can still speak about happiness and meaning et al., but she has become incapable of feeling anything in them, of understanding anything about them. Everything becomes an outline of the thing. Objects become schemata. The world becomes a map of the world.[18]

---

17 *Infinite Jest.*, 812.
18 Ibid., 210.

Kate Gompert, Hal, Joelle and various other characters all suffer the same fate. Their lived-experience becomes something "abstract" and separate from themselves. "The world becomes a map of the world." This is the fate of the postmodern ironist. One attempts to adopt the impossible perspective of an observer who theorises about her own experience. As Wallace shows, the perspective of the ironist is purely "negative," it empties the world of any significance whatsoever; 'understanding' is reduced to linguistic expression. Meaning is reduced to something which is conceptual and distant. Wallace identifies and attempts to write against the reduction of lived-experience to some static "thing."

Wallace's attempt to overcome the cultural/theoretical reification of lived-experience can be further illuminated by turning to the hermeneutic phenomenology of Heidegger. This reading offers a way to think about subjectivity and meaning without reducing either of these things to something static, objectified and "distant." Heideggerian phenomenology focuses on what is immediate to us, that is, lived-experience. A consideration of Heidegger's philosophy can offer an alternative to the theoretical presupposition that one can take one's own lived-experience as an object of reflection. For Heidegger, in opposition to Rorty, propositional language is not the source of meaning. We are born into a world which is already meaningful to us. For Heidegger, the structure of our human existence is Being-in-the-world.[19] We relate to and engage with things in terms of a broader, meaningful context. "World," in the Heideggerian sense, is the meaningful world of our lived-experience; not a world of isolated objects, but the very context that "structures" our lived-experience. This conception offers a different understanding of our relationship to meaning by emphasizing the priority of our everyday, meaningful engagement with things over our theoretical observation of them. "Meaning" is not something which we attach to things via the predicates of language, as Rorty has it, but is something which we already live in. For Heidegger, "existing is always factical … is always factically dependent on a definite 'world.'"[20] This conception of "world" escapes the "postmodern trap" outlined by Wallace whereby we would reduce existence to language.
With Heidegger we can think of our lived-experience without the distance of theoretical self-reflection by emphasising our hermeneutic *understanding*. For Heidegger, to theorise about something as an object of reflection removes that some*thing* from the broader meaningful context of our lives. The position of the ironist, reflecting on lived-experience as an "outsider" is already a

---

19 Heidegger, Martin. *Being and Time* (J. Stambaugh, trans.). SUNY P, 2010.
20 Ibid., 285.

theoretical approach. We do not "see" our "self" in our lived-experience. This understanding is comparable to Heidegger's concept of the "theoretical attitude" which is "possible only as a destruction of the environmental experience."[21] We cannot take something as complex as human lived-experience and single out something like language or "consciousness" which could then be observed and reflected upon, separate from our meaningful human context. Life is always *lived* and, therefore, can never be "theoretically known or conceptualized."[22] The self-aware ironist seeks to theorise about their life as if from the outside, making it the object of their examining gaze. The theoretical presupposition behind this way of seeing is that we can stand outside of our own lived-experiences of the surrounding world. On this account, our lived-experience supposedly becomes something which we can reflect on as a reified subject, something "outside" of our actual "living."[23] Our meaningful human life is always *lived*, that is, engaged with others and the "world."[24]

The theoretical "third-person" perspective of the ironist is an impossible one. The objectifying act of interminable self-reflection separates the ironist from the social world in which we live, but this position must still proceed, first and foremost, from this social world. It is a fundamentally problematic understanding of the self. The postmodern ironist is trapped in existential solipsism created by this position of total negativity. One simply cannot separate one*self* from the world. We cannot assume the position of an outsider to our own lives. The self-reflection of the ironist is an abstraction from the "life-world," that is, from one's "lived-experience" of the social world. Hal's attempt at reflecting on his initial lived-experience as a theoretical "object" is highlighted by Wallace as a necessarily endless and ultimately empty approach. Our life does not allow for an "outside" perspective. There can be no view that does not presuppose a world. Illustrative of this problem, Wallace presents the reader with various, often absurd, paradoxes. The self-reflective characters, who take lived-experience as theoretical, are completely paralysed by these paradoxes. One such example is Steve Erdedy, who is trapped, unable to move as he waits for his drug dealer because someone is at the door *and* the phone is ringing. Our life, living in a meaningful world, engaged with things, is

---

21 Heidegger, Martin. *Towards the Definition of Philosophy*. Continuum International Publishing Group, 2002, 67.
22 Von Herrmann, Friedrich-Wilhelm. *Hermeneutics and Reflection: Heidegger and Husserl on the Concept of Phenomenology*. U of Toronto P, 2013, xxxiii.
23 Ibid., 135–136.
24 Ibid., 17.

not something that can be theoretically known or "solved" from the outside. It is always *lived*.

Wallace's fiction is not, I argue, merely an attempt to dramatise or offer its own ironically critical account of irony but is an attempt to overcome this understanding by exposing the reader to what is overlooked by the ironist: our lived-experience which is already meaningful. It is here that I suggest that Heidegger can offer a unique approach to this problem. In his early work, Heidegger makes an important distinction between inauthentic and authentic existence. One finds oneself "thrown" into a "world" with others. Primarily and for the most part one is lost in "the they" or *das Man*. One understands oneself in terms of the possibilities of existence that circulate in the current "normal" and public interpretation of oneself.[25] For example, we are *thrown* into a certain gender which we understand ourselves in terms of. To question this every-day understanding that we live in, an understanding passed on by tradition, one must realise that one is responsible for one's life. One must grasp one's *own* possibility *from* this received interpretation. The structure of "fallenness" is inescapable, as is our involvement with *das Man*.[26] We can never be independent of our involvement with the world which is always-already shaped by one's "throwness." Heidegger offers a way to think about our individual mortal existence without relying on the problematic Rortian notion of total individual "redescription." Importantly, Heidegger's notion of authenticity does not imply anything like a static "essence" to selfhood to which our actions should conform.[27] Human beings are, for Heidegger, always "becoming."[28] We are finite beings who are thrown into a contingent situation which is inescapable.

The ironist is aware of the contingency of "self" and has fought her way to freedom, albeit to one completely empty. The freedom implied in the self-distance of irony is an impossible position. The ironist's awareness of the historical contingency sets her apart from others and keeps her in her self-

---

[25] Sheehan, Thomas; Painter, Corinne. "Choosing one's fate: A re-reading of Sein und Zeit (section) 74". *Research in phenomenology*; Proquest Religion; 1999, 63.

[26] Sheehan, Thomas. *Making Sense of Heidegger: A Paradigm Shift*. New Heidegger Research, 2015.

[27] Heidegger's concept of authenticity avoids the argument that the ideal of authenticity seems to imply the cohesion between one's actions and a "deeper" "core self" which would lead to self-reflection. See: Kelly, Adam. "David Foster Wallace and the New Sincerity in American Fiction." *Consider David Foster Wallace: Critical Essays*. Sideshow Media Group, 2010, 131–146.

[28] "Choosing one's fate: A re-reading of Sein und Zeit (section) 74," 71.

imposed solipsism. The ironist's rejection is empty, the position of theoretically "watching" oneself from the "outside" only leads to Hal's "analysis paralysis." Hal is incapable of embracing his own meaningful life because he is trapped in solipsism. He has adopted a third-person perspective and is paralysed by it. This condition can be connected to Wallace's focus on the postmodern ironist's inability to care or choose anything outside of the self. As one of the characters in *Infinite Jest* identifies, "I feel I am chained in a cage of the self…Unable to care or choose anything outside it."[29] Ironic detachment only works to separate the individual from the world of meaning, meaning whose foundation is not a creation of the self and never can be. This is why Rorty's ironist cannot achieve the individual "freedom" which he sees in "redescription." Irony is a purely negative movement; it can, perhaps, bring one to question one's inherited tradition, opening up the possibility of an authentic attitude, though it cannot, in itself, lead one to embrace an authentic existence. Authenticity requires openness to and responsibility for, the meaning found only in the world.[30]

The character who seems to best represent the attitude which can overcome the emptiness of the ironic attitude is Don Gately, who is able to embrace the meaningful world in authentic resoluteness. The saving grace for Gately is the "Alcoholics Anonymous" program which various characters are all struggling through. Wallace is at pains to show that the "AA" program is verifiably not anything like a metaphysical doctrine which provides one with a solution to the problem of this self-reflective introverted gaze. As Gately puts it, "You can't think about it like an intellectual thing…. You can analyse it til you're breaking tables with your forehead… Or you can stay and hang in and do the best you can."[31] The "AA" members are repeatedly described as "returned to themselves," that is, I suggest, returned to lived-experience. "AA" opens up a space for the paralysed, drug-addicted characters where they begin to understand that they cannot empty the world of meaning or of others. For Gately, this realisation saves him.

The individual in this culture of irony must not attempt to stand outside of one's "fallen self" but must accept one's responsibility for oneself and others and see them not as others which we manipulate but as people we live with. For Heidegger, authentic resoluteness means that we are open to our mortality by realising that our possibilities are limited. We cannot do everything. We must be willing to take responsibility for our finite life in the thrown

---

29 *Infinite Jest*, 777.
30 *Being and Time*, 285.
31 *Infinite Jest*, 1002.

situation. Heidegger insists that there is no doctrine which would outline which possibilities we *should* choose forever and always. He offers a formal structure of how we *might* take responsibility for our inherited "possibility" by overcoming the "rule" of tradition. Life is our own possibility as something which is always *lived*: it is not a static object but always dependent on one's active *living* in a particular historical situation; therefore, we must be *responsible* for the way we live.

In other words, we must take responsibility for our actions, realising that we live in a meaningful world that is not our creation; in recognising our finite freedom, we must assume responsibility for ourselves and for the human world which we are always involved with. Authenticity is opened up for the characters in "AA" because they are returned to the meaningful world after experiencing the "anhedonia" of irony's total breakdown of one's given meaning. Wallace makes it particularly clear that the AA slogans are not doctrine which can be theoretically understood; rather, they are something that must be *lived* through. Erdedy, trapped in the choice between phone and door, simply needs to act and be responsible for that action. *Solvitur ambulando*: The problem is solved by walking. The recovering addicts are directed back to the meaningful world for which they are now responsible, both for themselves and for others. This is not an easy task and, much like the addict, it's something one must be resolved to live with. Authenticity is not a goal which can finally be reached. One's life as contingent and always "becoming" is an end in itself. In resolute authenticity one does not negate the meaningful world but embraces one's responsibility to "choose one's fate."[32]

Utilising Heidegger's insights, my reading of *Infinite Jest* offers a unique approach to the existential problems faced by the ironist as represented in Wallace's fiction. I argue that Wallace's attempt to write through the problem of postmodern irony is not an issue which is confined to communication or language. Postmodern irony reinforces a cultural understanding of selfhood as some "thing" which can be grasped in reflection. Wallace argues that contemporary culture has "absorbed" thinking that was initially a linguistic theory, namely, postmodern irony. With Heidegger, we can re-think the idea of reflection without the theoretical presupposition that one can reflect on one*self*. I suggest that Heidegger's concept of authenticity, with a particular stress on *responsibility*, can illuminate Wallace's solution to the cultural problem which he identifies.

---

32 "Choosing one's fate: A re-reading of Sein und Zeit (section) 74," 73.

Works Cited

Boswell, Marshall. *Understanding David Foster Wallace*. U of South Carolina, 2003.

Colebrook, Claire. *Irony*. Routledge, 2004.

De Man. Paul. *Blindness and Insight: Essays in the Rhetoric of Contemporary Criticism*. Methuen, 1983.

Heidegger, Martin. *Being and Time*. Translated by J. Stambaugh, SUNY P, 2010.

-- -- --. *Towards the Definition of Philosophy*. Continuum International Publishing Group, 2002.

Kelly, Adam. "David Foster Wallace and the New Sincerity in American Fiction." *Consider David Foster Wallace: Critical Essays*. Sideshow Media Group, 2010, 131–146.

McCaffery, Larry. "An Interview with David Foster Wallace." *Review of Contemporary Fiction*. 13 (2), 1993: 127–150.

Rorty, Richard. *Contingency, Irony and Solidarity*. Cambridge UP, 1989.

-- -- --. *Philosophy and the mirror of nature*. Princeton UP, 1979.

Sheehan, Thomas. *Making Sense of Heidegger: A Paradigm Shift*. New Heidegger Research, 2015.

Sheehan, Thomas; Painter, Corinne. "Choosing one's fate: A re-reading of Sein und Zeit (section) 74." *Research in phenomenology*; Proquest Religion; 1999, 63-82.

Von Herrmann, Friedrich-Wilhelm. *Hermeneutics and Reflection: Heidegger and Husserl on the Concept of Phenomenology*. U of Toronto P, 2013.

Wallace, David Foster. "E Unibus Pluram: Television and U.S. Fiction." *Review of Contemporary Fiction*. 13.2. 1993: 151–194.

-- -- --. *Infinite Jest*. London: Abacus, 1997.

Wittgenstein, Ludwig. *Philosophical Investigations*. Cengage Gale, 1973.

Is an Antidepressant a Ramp or a Prosthesis? The Nonendogenous Literature of David Foster Wallace

Rhett Farinholt

> *The Bad Thing—which I guess is really depression—is very different, and indescribably worse.*—David Foster Wallace, "The Planet Trillaphon as it Stands in Relation to the Bad Thing"

The trajectory of recent attention to the works of David Foster Wallace offers a rough but useful analogue to the rise of disability studies within the academy over the last few decades, and the synthesis of these two ascendant projects is an important and fruitful nexus for investigation. Wallace is not just an important writer, but an important writer for disability studies. Certainly, some of Wallace's import to disability studies draws from his biography. Wallace's lengthy struggles with addiction and depression, his dependence on the MAOI antidepressant Nardil (Phenelzine), his experiences with electroconvulsive therapy, and the unhappy fact of his suicide all paint Wallace as a *disabled* writer, but just as important as his biography are the configurations of disability within the fiction he produced. This focus has resulted in some very promising critical work. Emily Russell has explored the grotesque "assemblages" of disabled bodies in Wallace's magnum opus *Infinite Jest*, particularly in relation to her idea of "embodied citizenship," to argue for "he necessary interdependence of textual, social, and physical body in imagining modern American democracy" (3). Mental disability has been a useful lens for Matt Tresco who has considered "autism as a narrative form" (114) in *Infinite Jest*. Thomas Tracey's reading of trauma in Wallace's short story collection *Oblivion* stands out as perhaps the closest link between disability studies and Wallace's short fiction, but even that tenuous connection requires that one traverse the "discursive abyss [of]…mutual exclusion" (Berger 563) that James Berger posits between the fields of trauma and disability studies. While scholars have made some significant inroads in the last decade, there is still a great deal of unexamined work in Wallace's oeuvre that can benefit from a thorough application of the tools developed within the field of disability studies.

This paper is taken from a larger project that is structured around the critical reading of three keywords that broaden our ability to understand various disabilities, and reassert literature's vital role in the processes of community building, empathy, and visibility that are crucial to the proper function of a heterogeneous society composed of individuals with a wide variety of embodiments and mental experiences. A critical disability reading of literary texts gives us the tools to think through the complexities of physical impairment, psychoanalytical treatment, and psychopharmacology, intervening in what are too often viewed as purely scientific interactions. In the larger project from which this paper derives, I conduct three critical readings of the fiction of David Foster Wallace by organizing my analyses according to the labeling information for Wallace's MAOI antidepressant, Nardil (Phenelzine). According to Nardil's FDA indications, the drug is "found to be effective in depressed patients clinically characterized as 'atypical,' 'nonendogenous,' or 'neurotic'" (Parke-Davis). These three categories, "atypical," "nonendogenous," and "neurotic," provide the headings for my larger project's readings of Wallace's fiction, from which I draw the keyword for this essay: "Nonendogenous."

As a term through which to analyze the discourses of disability at play in the fiction of David Foster Wallace, "nonendogenous" presents an interesting challenge, particularly in terms of definition. Nonendogenous is such a sheltered, clinical word that it does not even have an entry in the Oxford English Dictionary; instead, the term is almost always defined against "endogenous," which in psychiatric practice refers to "disorders originating within the individual" (*OED*). Like so many terms in the psychiatric field, nonendogenous is a source of great clinical and theoretical debate. In the scientific literature on the differential diagnosis of endogenous and nonendogenous depression[1], it is not uncommon to encounter uncharacteristically ambivalent statements like, "[s]ome psychiatrists see no basic difference between the symptoms of the two forms of illness, whereas others are convinced that a sharp distinction exists" (Matussek & Luks 235), or "[f]or many years, a major area of debate has centered around the endogenous and nonendogenous states, particularly their relationship and their criteria for definition" (Schatzberg 3). Clearly the psychiatric community's use of the term "nonendogenous" is fluid and open to the critical manipulation required of an application to literary readings.

---

[1] The initial distinction between these terms is widely attributed to German titan of scientific psychiatry Emil Kraepelin, whose work in the late 19th and early 20th century was instrumental in the classification of mental illness. It should also be noted that Kraepelin loudly opposed the types of mistreatment common to psychiatric asylums of the era, yet was also an enthusiastic supporter of eugenics and racial hygiene.

Given this flexibility and debate in definition, I will focus my interpretation of the word nonendogenous to refer to that which originates outside of the body, from the environment. From this position I will look at the work of Rosemary Garland-Thomson, engaging with her materialist feminist disability concept of "misfit" to examine how her environmental understanding of disability can offer new insight into abnormal mental experience and its pharmaceutical treatment. After demarcating the critical terrain for such an analysis, I will close this section by applying my readings of nonendogenous and misfit to David Foster Wallace's short story "The Planet Trillaphon as it Stands in Relation to the Bad Thing" (1984), arguing that such literature offers one of the only avenues for a reconciliation of the celebration of visual disability as a welcome symbol of human variation with the inability to visually express mental disabilities.

In developing a literary reading of the nonendogenous, I first turn to Rosemary Garland-Thomson's critical keyword "misfit," which she defines as "a consideration of how the particularities of embodiment interact with the environment in its broadest sense, to include both spatial and temporal aspects" (592). Garland-Thomson's misfitting shifts the focus in situations of disjunction or incongruence away from the individual and onto the dynamic juxtaposition of a specific body and a specific environment. Thus the discursive material utility of misfitting is to emphasize "context over essence, relation over isolation, [and] mediation over origination" (593). According to this conceptual framework, a person with an impairment that requires a wheelchair is not disabled until she encounters an unsustaining environment that lacks ramps or elevators; the trouble inheres not in the individual but in the misfit between body and world. Garland-Thomson's application of "misfit" allows her to engage with a number of feminist materialist conversations, such as those on dependence, vulnerability, and performativity, ultimately reconfirming the fundamental position of disability politics that "social justice and equal access should be achieved by changing the shape of the world, not changing the shape of our bodies...[that the disabled] should be provided with sustaining environments that allow them to participate fully as equal citizens rather than urging them toward normalization through medical scientific cure" (597).

"Misfit" gives us an extraordinarily useful tool for thinking through the complexities that result from a disjunctive meeting between body and environment, but Garland-Thomson's focus is exclusively trained on physical disability, predominantly the kind that registers visually in the social environment. "Misfitting," Garland-Thomson asserts, "ignites a vivid recognition of our fleshliness and the contingencies of human embodiment" (597-98).

By focusing on "our fleshliness," Garland-Thomson's work does not explicitly consider the various misfits and disjunctions between the individual and her environment that occur within the scope of mental disability. How, for example, might we examine the misfit of environmental barriers that excludes the depressed, clinically anxious, or psychotic from full participation as equal citizens? Are there mental or psychiatric analogues for the stairs, ramps and elevators of the built environment? Furthermore, what role does psychopharmacology play in the disability politics discourse of resistance toward "normalization through medical scientific cure"? Does a pill that mitigates disabling feelings of anxiety or depression serve to "normalize" a person's brain, or does it act on that person's perception of an unsustaining environment? Is an antidepressant a prosthesis or a ramp?

These questions can be best explored by adding considerations of mental disability and variation of mental experience to Garland-Thomson's "misfit." I call the result of this process the nonendogenous. There are, of course, a few problems[2] in reconciling "misfit" with the particular environmental issues specific to mental disabilities[3]. Mental disability does not immediately present on the visual register, nor is a mentally disabled person likely to find herself misfitting with the built environment in ways that "changing the shape of the world," as Garland-Thomson sees it, could help. When Rosemarie Garland-Thomson cites Linda Martín Alcoff's work to suggest that we "make identities more visible" (597) to construct a positive narrative around human variation, she highlights a potential source of great political agency, but also risks alienating those whose disabilities are difficult to make more visible, or, indeed, those whose very disability is related to the psychic distress of their own visibility. It is precisely here, in the gap between Garland-Thomson's fleshly misfitting, and the invisible disability of the nonendogenous, that literature, and perhaps the arts more generally, can intervene. Literature's power to express mental experience, to connect the consciousnesses of the reader and author, and to make visible the invisible make it uniquely suited to taking up the challenge of constructing a positive narrative around the wide variation of human experience in the invisible realm of the mind. A nonendogenous literary theory then, would help reshape the misfit between "misfit" and mental disability.

---

2 Theoretical "misfits," you could say.
3 Not the least of these concerns is the view, held by Lennard Davis among others, that people with "mild to moderate depression" (Davis, *End of Normal*, 44) should not be considered disabled at all. While Davis raises some provocative points regarding the classification of these conditions, surely he would concede that the suicidal depression shared by David Foster Wallace and the narrator of "The Planet Trillaphon…" would exceed the "mild to moderate" threshold of a disabling mental condition.

To develop this nonendogenous literary theory I'd like to look at David Foster Wallace's earliest short story, "The Planet Trillaphon as it Stands in Relation to the Bad Thing," published in 1984 in the Amherst Review when the author was still an undergraduate. Almost totally ignored by scholars so far, Wallace's first published story displays a number of characteristics that would come to define the author's style: exceedingly long, maximalist syntax; a vernacular and colloquial voice delivered with exacting grammatical precision; and an obsession with the communication of abnormal mental experience. While clearly the product of a young, developing writer[4], "The Planet Trillaphon…" is a great example of how literature, and Wallace's work in particular, can communicate the thorny environmental problems of invisible disability and its psychopharmaceutical treatment. The "Bad Thing" of the story's lengthy title is depression, and the "Planet Trillaphon" is the narrator's imagining of the altered state he lives in on antidepressants after a failed suicide attempt ("Trillaphon" itself being the narrator's intentional misremembering of the name of his antidepressant, Tofranil, an early tri-cyclic). This imaginary construction of a psychopharmacologically sustaining environment starts in the story's first lines:

> I've been on antidepressants for, what, about a year now, and I suppose I feel as if I'm pretty qualified to tell what they're like. They're fine, really, but they're fine in the same way that, say, living on another planet that was warm and comfortable and had food and fresh water would be fine: it would be fine, but it wouldn't be good old Earth, obviously. I haven't been on Earth now for almost a year, because I wasn't doing very well on Earth. I've been doing somewhat better here where I am now, on the planet Trillaphon, which I suppose is good news for everyone involved. (26)

The narrator's opening analogy between being on antidepressants and living on a different, though similar, planet literalizes and recontextualizes the misfit between body and world. The shape of the world cannot be changed, but the world itself can be switched out through the intervention of antidepressants, though this comes at the cost of alienation and isolation from "everyone involved." Wallace's planet-swapping image here provides a rich and evocative counter to the longstanding claim of the medical and pharmaceutical communities that antidepressants bring the brain's function back to "normal" by correcting a "chemical imbalance[5]." Instead, Wallace's opening suggests a nonendogenous alteration, a "somewhat better" change to the *perception* of

---

4 See, for example, the name of the narrator's love interest, May Aculpa, a sobriquet so on-the-nose that it almost reads as a satire of Thomas Pynchon.
5 For a scientific counter to the chemical imbalance hypothesis, see Irving Kirsch's meta-analysis of early antidepressant clinical trials in *The Emperor's New Drugs* (2009).

the narrator's environment, but not the "normalization" of a brain deficient in a certain chemical. In this instance, it seems clear that Tofranil operates as a ramp and not a prosthesis.

Extending this nonendogenous reading of "The Planet Trillaphon…" we might look at the problems specific to a misfit between the depressed patient and the environment. As Garland-Thomson points out, "[t]he primary negative effect of misfitting is exclusion from the public sphere—a literal casting out—and the resulting segregation into domestic spaces or sheltered institutions" (594). This segregation obviously removes the misfitting person from public visibility, but also attaches the stigma of institutionalization to the individual. In the case of the institutionalized "mental patient," this stigma participates in a lengthy tradition of infantilization[6] and feminization that has historically been imposed on the mentally ill. Wallace's short story allows us to see this process at work after the narrator is committed to "The White Floor" of the hospital after a failed suicide attempt. It is hard to ignore the tone of infantilization and feminization behind the narrator's recollection that, "everything about the White Floor was soft and unimposing and…*demure*" (31, ellipsis and italics in original) and that "the White Floor smelled a lot nicer than the rest of the hospital, all feminine and dreamy" (31). This infantilization and feminization extends to the types of food served on the White Floor ("Pudding was a very big item" (31)), the control over potentially dangerous items like matches, and even to the built environment itself. Commenting on the absurdity of all the beveled and rounded off corners and edges of the furniture on the White Floor, Wallace's narrator says, "I have never heard of anyone trying to kill himself on the sharp corner of a door, but I suppose it is wise to be prepared for all possibilities" (31).

In connecting a mental disability like depression to Garland-Thomson and Alcoff's call for increased visibility as a community building strategy within disability, another problem develops around the ontological differences between the mentally and physically disabled. A physically disabled person can celebrate her worth and value as a person while simultaneously acknowledging that her impairment requires an alternative environment to ensure a proper fit. For certain mental disabilities though, the misfit is, in some sense, between the self and the very idea of worth and value as a person. How does one celebrate a self that represents human variation, when that variation is fundamentally hostile to the self? The narrator of "The Planet Trillaphon…" grapples with

---

6 S. Weir Mitchell's famous "rest cure," in the early 20th century, for example, treated those diagnosed with hysteria or neurasthenia by prohibiting work of any kind, and, among other things, cutting the patient's food into small pieces as you might for a child.

precisely this dilemma in attempting to describe the paradoxes of "the Bad Thing" that is depression. "The way to fight against or get away from the Bad Thing is clearly just to think differently, to reason and argue with yourself, just to change the way you're perceiving and sensing and processing stuff. But you need your mind to do this]…and that's exactly what the Bad Thing has made too sick to work right . . . you are the sickness yourself" (29). Here lies one of the fundamental difficulties in covering the physically and mentally disabled under a single theoretical structure: one is a person who endures an impairment, the other is a person who is the impairment to be endured. In the case of Wallace's depressed narrator, the environment that needs changing is the shadowy interior architecture of the self, the apparatus that handles all the "perceiving and sensing and processing" from without. Such a setup is not written visually on the body, nor is it immediately relatable in a summary of symptoms or a meta-analysis of clinical trials. Neither the scientific nor the psychiatric community can communicate this fundamental disjunction with nearly the precision and power of a work of literature. If visibility and empathy are crucial to the disability politics of developing more fitting environments, then there can be no more important tool in bringing such an agenda to invisible disabilities than the literature of the nonendogenous.

Works Cited

Berger, James. "Trauma Without Disability, Disability Without Trauma: A Disciplinary Divide." *Journal of Advanced Composition* 24.3 (2004), 563-82.

Davis, Lennard. *The End of Normal: Identity in a Biocultural Era*. Ann Arbor: U of Michigan P, 2014.

"endogenous, adj." *OED Online*. Oxford UP, December 2015. Accessed 10 Feb. 2016.

Garland-Thomson, Rosemarie. "Integrating Disability, Transforming Feminist Theory." *The Disability Studies Reader*. Ed. Lennard J. Davis. 4th ed. Routledge, 2013, 333-53.

Kirsch, Irving. *The Emperor's New Drugs: Exploding the Antidepressant Myth*. Basic, 2009.

Matussek, P., and O. Luks. "Themes of Endogenous and Nonendogenous Depressions." *Beiträge Zur Psychodynamik Endogener Psychosen* 5 (1981): 235-42. *Springer*. Accessed 10 Feb. 2016.

Parke-Davis, a Division of Pfizer, Inc. "Nardil Patient Package Insert." New York: https://www.accessdata.fda.gov/drugsatfda_docs/label/2007/011909s038lbl.pdf, 2007. Accessed 8 September 2015.

Russell, Emily. *Reading Embodied Citizenship*. Rutgers UP, 2011.

Schatzberg, Alan. "Classification of Depressive Disorder." *Depression: Biology, Psychodynamics, and Treatment*. Ed. J. Cole. Plenum, 1978. Springer. Accessed 10 Feb. 2016.

Tracey, Thomas. "Representations of Trauma in David Foster Wallace's *Oblivion*." *Consider David Foster Wallace: Critical Essays*. Ed. David Hering. Sideshow Media Group, 2010. 172-86.

Tresco, Matt. "Impervious to U.S. Parsing: Encyclopedism, Autism, and *Infinite Jest*." *Consider David Foster Wallace: Critical Essays*. Ed. David Hering. Sideshow Media Group Press, 2010. 113-22.

Wallace, David Foster. "The Planet Trillaphon as it Stands in Relation to the Bad Thing." *The Amherst Review* XII (1984). 26-33.

from *Zuzu's Petals*
Jeff Jarot

I pull up and exit my vehicle.

In order to reach the building from the parking lot, which is an obscene distance from the school, I cross a bridge that suspends a small body of water that is barely frozen.

A transparent wafer of ice covers the surface of the water.

Only in the movies would someone be able to safely hop across its surface, Gene Kelly-like, without breaking through to experience hypothermia's bitter embrace.

Without realizing it, I have stopped in the middle of the bridge, head down, hands clasped.

When I finally look up, my watering eyes decipher a man and a woman holding hands.

They offer me a sidelong glance. Their crystal orbs scream, "What is *that* guy's problem?"

I follow their silhouettes like a humiliated shadow towards the welcoming light of the school.

Even though my mind has already jumped from the side of the bridge to its early death, my feet follow the receding figures in their shared wake towards the building in which Zuzu's holiday program awaits.

I'm not ashamed to say that I, Jules, prefer Fiction to Reality.

Fiction will become the Official Reality of record.

Julie and I are still together.

Zuzu will always be my little girl.

We are a happy family and always will be.

***

Something's wrong with mommy and daddy.

They won't tell me what.

Butterflies in my stomach are making babies.

Butterflies being born every second.

Wait a minute.

Butterflies are worms before they're even butterflies.

Maybe I have worms in my stomach.

Maybe I have worms *and* butterflies.

There's lots of people out there.

There's mommy.

I want to go on.

Where's daddy?

***

I'm here.

I enter the building. To my right is a chiffarobe-sized glass display case. Back in the day it housed two plaques that meant something to me. Amidst the militarily-precise rows and columns of dusty rectangles of gold, my own name was etched for pseudo-eternity, quasi-memorialized in half-inch capital block letters. These plaques and others like them were long ago removed from the case to make room for future elementary school alumni, my scholarly descendants, and the old, irrelevant plaques no doubt were burned in a bonfire or sent to decompose in a landfill or a graveyard especially designed for the purpose. Who knows?

The gymnasium in which the holiday program will be performed hasn't changed much. You don't relocate a huge, cavernous indoor expanse like that if you can help it. Why would you want to? It hasn't been refurbished, which adds to my feeling of having been transported through time, if not for the ubiquitous presence of camcorders, smart phones, digital cameras, and all manner of electronic device.

My mind courses back to 1981. The school administration has decided to shut off the heat to the gym in an attempt to prevent random upchucks and faintings. This executive decision results in a Celsius reading inside the gym that is consistent with the interior of a walk-in freezer on the ice-planet Hoth. I feel the tingle of goose pimples metastasize on my forearms like pinhead tumors with arm hairs standing erect at attention when I enter the maw of the gym's gaping wooden double doors.

But it is the present, and the temperature, like everything else in my life, is lukewarm.

Jesus, what I would do to be a kid again. These kids don't know how easy they have it.

The annual elementary school dramatic-musical extravaganza usually consists of both select instrumental and choral performances. A cranberry-colored partition that separates the music room from the gym is cracked open and retracted to accommodate all the performers. The band students and those, like my Zuzu, who are performing piano selections, are housed in the music room. There is a set of risers in the shape of a crescent moon knocked on its side near the front of the makeshift stage. Here the students who are singing can belt out carols in cacophonous unison.

When I was a student here, the overcast-sky floor tiles and bright yellow lines demarcating the basketball court dimensions always reminded me of elongated and curving blocks of lemon-meringue filling floating on top of speckled, dirty dishwater. The canary-colored rectangles didn't undulate but rather were motionless, as if the grey liquid was in a calm pool undisturbed by wind. I recall pretending that these lines and dashes were haven-like, foot-sized islands and tightropes of safety strung across the stormcloud-colored boiling waters that seethed just below. Black streaks courtesy of various student gym footwear stops and starts and scuffs and slides floated on the surface. They are still floating there, but my mind tells my body that it is too old to spring out of its seat to see if its skills at hopping across the tiled maelstrom have suffered across the chasm of the intervening decades.

The squiggly nature of the design of the room's ceiling tiles always reminded me of unwieldy piles of spaghetti on a tuxedo-black background, as if gravity had been reversed and, were it to be restored, I would tumble headlong into piles of pasta that would cushion the fall. The ceiling is held up by bone-white girders.

This forces me to contemplate the invisible girders that hold up life.

They can crumble at any moment, like they are memories made of mist, misremembered.

In my long-deceased elementary school day, in this very building, during this particular breed of holiday program that I am about to witness as a member of the audience, the heater would be running full blast to counter the early-December outside elements. Combined with the formidable number of teachers, students, and proud parents packed into the enclosed space like superheated sardines boiling in their own juices, this made for extremely sweltering conditions. Not a holiday season would go by without a handful of spotlit students succumbing to the intense heat, fainting and tumbling off the risers or, worse, becoming physically ill and losing their noon repast the hard way.

The lights dim and the program starts. In the gloaming I can make out the empty rack where battleship-grey folding chairs will need to be racked upside-down one after the other post-program. I am already anticipating the end.

Zuzu is the very first student to perform. She plays a simple rendition of "O Christmas Tree" that is free of complicated chord structures. I've heard variations of the piece off and on for the last couple months, smooth patches interrupted by avant-gardish interludes of sudden discordant musical constructs produced by Zuzu's frustration.

Back in our homestead, hearing her work her way through these microcosmic struggles, I felt the water wells of my eyes fill up, and I'm afraid that presently they are on the verge of overflowing their teary juices like aggressively-squeezed orbs of fruit. These homegrown rivulets will be recognized immediately by the strangers surrounding me. Forthwith when they recall this event I'll be remembered as "that strange stranger with the tear-stained face. Remember that poor, sorry bastard? What was his problem?"

***

I notice a smattering of fallen, shriveling, probably dying crimson-with-a-blight-of-brown poinsettia leaves garnishing the polished ebony top of the piano on which Zuzu is playing. Her performance is followed by that of an olive-skinned student with a bowl haircut clad in a black T-shirt emblazoned with the large, ivory, block letters "FBI" (I discover upon closer examination after the recital they stand for "Female Body Inspector"). He clutches a French horn to his belly and farts and splurts his way through what I think is Alan Silvestri's theme from *The Polar Express*. The lad sounds like an outboard boat motor that is running out of gas. Performing next is a scrum of chittering first graders who, after stomping up and across the risers, belt out a wildly-out-of-tune rendition of "Silent Night." The young ones commence the second chorus, murmuring with not nearly the confidence the first verse exuded.

Midway through the next selection, I hear liquid splatting onto tile, followed by EEEEEEEWWWWWWWWWWWWWWWWWW!!!!!

It is just enough to cause my lips to curve up at the edges. Tears pause at the precipice of my lower eyelids, and they decide to not jump off the cliff.

God, oh God, it's starting.

In my lap, a bouquet of flowers for Zuzu lies wilting. It is an assortment of white, pink, and red roses.

My and Julie's given names have always served as a trigger for much mirth and comment between friends and new acquaintances alike. The similarity of the monikers our respective parents gave us has caused many a colleague to comment that Julie's and my high-school romance, college courtship, and subsequent marriage was pre-ordained, inscribed in the stars and planets whirling above.

Star-cross'd lovers, indeed.

Utter garbage, when all was said and done.

Well, it would be more accurate to say that it's in the process of being done.

I'm perched on a weatherworn picnic table, a collection of splinters dappled with rust-colored paint, held together by the inertia of time. It's unreasonably warm for December 10th, and Zuzu is sprinting from the table to a beanbag-chair-sized mound of damp leaves the color of cranberries and black-bean soup.

The innocence of youth. How to get back to it?

Yet the doomsday clock on her innocence is speedily, inexorably winding down to zero. I'll have to break the news to her very soon. But I don't want to do it alone.

The days of my life churn in my mind like grains of sand beneath rolling, incessant waves. I want Zuzu's tinier footprints to be right there in the fresh unmarked sand next to mine as we stride forward.

I drop the needle on a copy of the Beach Boys' *Pet Sounds* I just acquired from Waiting Room Records. The Brian Wilson-penned harmonies tease and taunt me.

***

I am resigned to the fact that I'm nothing if not a lost cause. The fact that I'm listening to said song on a turntable highlights my plight, my inability to swim out of the old-school current in which I'm trapped. Yet vinyl *has* made a comeback of sorts for audiophiles, they say. And dammit, given that, why should I feel strange if I still prefer to read physical books as well? Why the devil do I have to perform some kind of army crawl past the employees at a bookstore who are hawking the latest version of some electronic reading device and causing their jobs to make that slow swirl down the toilet of oblivion in the process? Isn't it the content that matters anyways? Whether I listen to *Rubber Soul* on vinyl or CD or 8-track or a download, what does it matter? The greatness of the album will never change.

I cannot help myself. Like Brian Wilson, I feel as if I was born in the wrong era. And I hate a good portion of myself for it. I don't understand why I was conceived and birthed and raised in the very same decade that spawned Watergate and Jimmy Carter and disco and 8-tracks and…well…*Star Wars*.

Yet why do people nowadays feel compelled to take pictures of food they've either prepared or consumed? Why do they post innermost feelings that should be reserved for *real-life* moments of intimacy with another living, *present* human being? Because now they can ponder what to say and type it without uncomfortable, pregnant patches of silence and interminable stretches of waiting for a response and the glassy stares of the other person in a conversation in the *Now*, boring their own crystal orbs deep into the soul of another.

Simply stated, if you don't post it on Facebook or tweet about it nowadays, the event or thought doesn't and didn't happen because no one has read about it and seen the carefully-composed pictures and commented on them or otherwise enjoyed them. Hence, those events and thoughts that represent a life never occurred.

None of this is nourishing in any way for anyone. It's like eating candy corn for breakfast, lunch, and dinner day after day after day.

Was the secret to marry someone who had the very same obsessions that I have? How possible is that? Or maybe someone who obsesses on completely different things but at the same levels of intensity that I do? Did I fail to follow the dictum that opposites attract?

Do opposites even attract? I think maybe all they end up doing is pissing each other off. Or one person becomes colossally pissed while the other glides along.

    Like me.

"Spectral Apostrophe" and *The Inkiest Black*
Barbara Balfour

The introduction to my artist's book *The Inkiest Black* is also the introduction to the paper I'll read today. It's called, "Needs No Introduction."

Although ostensibly intended as a compliment, this expression invoked in the context of introducing a well-known figure can be a disappointing kind of disclaimer. Wouldn't the person in question actually merit a considered introduction?

And yet there are occasions when you might want to avoid a preface coloring one's experience of a person or thing. In the case of this particular book, I am hesitant to say too much from the outset. A lot depends upon whether or not you, the reader, are familiar with the life, work, and death of David Foster Wallace. (And in terms of this particular gathering, the familiarity with Wallace is certain.) If so, then this book might need no introduction. If not, then I hope that *The Inkiest Black* will act as a manicule, pointing you specifically to DFW's novel *Infinite Jest*.

I want to believe the fiction, in fiction, that the author is speaking directly to you, the reader. Even if I know it not to be true, I'm often convinced that it is.

To believe the author is engaging in a mode of address, even when the author is dead, would mean one believes in a kind of spectral mediation, albeit a purely literary one. Although I certainly knew DFW was not contacting me, in a version of counter-apostrophe, it didn't prevent me from replying.

ember-red
mercuric red
violently red
wet-nail-polish red
the dusky red of fire through much smoke
that pushy shade of Canadian red
an odd kind of red, as of old blood

My experience of reading David Foster Wallace's *Infinite Jest* was immersion punctuated by interruption. Certain words literally stopped me from reading further, with a frequency making it impossible to keep track of vocabulary. I realized I could not keep pointing to every word that caught my eye—I soon would have run out of fingers.

A pattern evolved: I began a list of words I knew and loved and then consulted the O.E.D. for certain words I didn't know, which I in turn recorded. The extraordinary range of DFW's lexicon—including Latin expressions, street slang, what appears to be willfully misspelled Québécois jargon, and certain 'Wallaceian' expressions and turns of phrases—leads the reader in myriad directions. Words such as "lume, snafu, orts, skirl, deliquesce, widow-webs, notebookish, intellectualish, and pastry-dependence," along with almost phrase-like hyphenated words such as "drenching-sweat-proof-ink, amanuensis-cum-operative, now-pretty-clearly-superfluous."

This fascination lead to my compiling almost nine hundred words in *Long List*, the first section of my artist's book *The Inkiest Black*. The impulse behind my noting down these words in the form of a list was not to produce a glossary but to savor them, in and out of the context of the novel, to hold on to them in a "vade mecumish" kind of way.

autumnal orange
citrus orange
the deep color of quality squash
rust-colored
the color of low flame

In the third section, "White, Black," in the sequential order and relative placement in which they appear in *IJ*, I arranged DFW's references to these two colors. I devised a system for preserving the sequence and order of these citations, condensing fifty pages of the novel into one page of my artist's book. As I became attentive to the color references in *Infinite Jest*, I realized that there were, in particular, a significant number of instances of 'black' and 'white', often in connection to mood and depressive states in the former, and to death and the grave, as well as tennis, in the latter. Many were unadorned by adjectives and other modifiers; others consisted of more suggestive phrases.

As with Wallace's extensive vocabulary in general and the idiosyncratic color references in particular, I found so many of the occurrences of the words 'white' and 'black' to be arresting. These interruptions struck me as similar to the way in which the sudden recognition of the graphic fact of letterforms in black ink on white paper can actually prevent one from reading. As a supplement of sorts to this larger project, I wanted to note and consider, admittedly excised from the narrative and clearly with *emphasis mine*, the varied instances of 'white' and 'black'. Ranging from single, unadorned words to detailed and elaborately modified terms and phrases, they end with one of my personal favorites, "the inkiest black."

jonquil yellow
the color of pallid cheese
urine-yellow
deep autumnal yellow
jaundice-yellow
onionskin yellow
burnt yellow

At some point in amassing the lexicon that became "Long List", I realized that the vocabulary encountered in *Infinite Jest* can engender any number of specific word lists, relating to tennis terminology or drug slang, for example. One such spinoff list, emerging out of my reading and derived from the subtly distinguished colors mentioned by Wallace, became the basis of "Qualified Colours," the middle section of my book.

I had noted a number of surprising and eloquent color descriptions I couldn't help but imagining. What would "obscene pink" or "burnt yellow" look like? Would I recognize "the white of long death?" Familiar with mixing printing ink, I decided to do just that with DFW's idiosyncratic, 'qualified' colors.

kind of nauseous dark-green
mint-green
the color of really old olives
indecisive green
the watery green of extreme ocean depths
deep deadwater gray-green

I made a working list of a subset of color citations, subsequently subdivided into a loosely based spectrum. Departing slightly from the ROYGBIV sequence of red, orange, yellow, green, blue, indigo, and violet (relating best to the spectra of light), I formed groups corresponding to red, orange, yellow, green, blue, pink/purple, brown, grey, white, and black. Each set included six or seven variations on a given hue.

deep glowing neutron-blue
pilot-light blue
vague robin's egg
aftershave-blue
milky blue
sky-blue
apothecary-blue

Although I had a notion in advance of some colors—"apothecary blue," "the color of pallid cheese," "the dusky red of fire through much smoke", I took artistic license with others—"furious purple," "creepy gray," "the slightly sad color of early winter P.M." The challenge of "indecisive green" was in producing a green that would raise doubt as to its own greenness; it couldn't be too self-assured or convincing. Caution had to be exercised to forestall a touch of red making a blue too purple, some yellow added to red causing it to veer toward orange and lose its very redness, a lightly tinted white swiftly becoming another color altogether. For each colour mixed there were numerous inky iterations, necessary precursors to the one best approximating, to my mind, a DFW color.

dusky rose
faint sick pink
obscene pink
chemically pink
darker violet
mature-eggplant-skin
furious purple

The practice of doing draw-downs, applying thin bands of printing ink onto paper with an ink knife, is well known to those working in print studios. A concentration of several grams of ink cannot convey how a single ink layer ultimately reveals itself when printed. Resembling commercial paint chips, draw-downs have a clear function: to indicate the full strength, level of transparency, and undertones of a given color when applied to paper, ideally the one on which one intends to print.

dusty brown
confectioner's rich brown
the color of strong tea
tannin-brown
deerskin-brown
linen-pale

Certain color sets, such as green and brown, allowed for a vast array of difference while nevertheless adhering to their respective categories. Other groupings posed certain challenges, such as the tenuous threshold of the reds, threatening to become at any moment either orange or brown. And yet the most nuanced distinctions were necessary in colors that might be expected to be more straightforward, those of black and white.

creepy gray
elephant-colored
dove-colored
the color of sand mixed with ash
dust-colored
rat-colored
the slightly sad color of early winter P.M.

Draw-downs are one instance of myriad technical steps tacitly taken in a print project. As print-based artifacts, they have long fascinated me in being more beautiful than technically necessary. They retain a paradoxically 'printerly' character without actually being printed. Nonetheless, draw-downs tend to be summarily discarded once they've served their function.

Tangible signs of the work to come, draw-downs are produced with a certain layer of an image to be printed in mind. When I began mixing the sixty-seven colors comprising "Qualified Colours," others working alongside me in the print studio took note. The assumption was that I was undertaking a large printing project, although with more colors than one would tend to mix, especially within a related range of hues. I had to explain that this work *was* the work, an end in itself.

clean-sheet-white
salt-white
white of the grave
the white of long death
anachronistic white
birch-colored
vampire-white

When the ten color sets were exhibited, viewers felt comfortable assessing their veracity and accuracy, voicing opinions on the more speculative propositions. Discussion ensued in particular about blues and greens, commonly disputed hues in terms of one being taken for the other. In the end, my draw-down color choices are undeniably subjective interpretations remaining open to debate, hopefully bearing some resemblance to the colors that were in the mind's eye of David Foster Wallace, yet never entirely becoming a case of black and white.

black as ink
glossy black
eyeliner-colored
pubic-black
bright-black
absolute blackness
the inkiest black

from "Exit Interview"
Jane L. Carman

Uncaged

His dreams hung thick on each syllable, vowels twisting together to strengthen the cord. Over the course thoughts bloomed, shriveled, resurfaced, and morphed into fantasies rich with tiny pains swelling as they traveled. Images fired: mother; friend; sister; lover; a black cube; a pony; a dog broken in half, connected only by red ropes; the hands of a boy, of a man, his own hands; words on bright white paper, "We are sorry to inform you that..."; a baby beached and wilting under fluorescent shame. Sounds long gone flowered: a woodpecker tapping on the elm; a lover's sigh; the sharpness of a shovel scrapping dead from pavement; a long, shrill note; the snap of a twisted ulna; the silence that follows concrete opening a skull.

      vowels strengthening the cord
            constants rapping and wrapping
                                  tightening

The dreams redefining. Desire melting into love. Love a myth, a fantastic devise. Respect a taunt, a lust lurking, spiked. His dreams spoke American: the ideal education, romance, holiday, vehicle, house.

    Anybody can   if only they   if only
        Any   body   and if a body can't

Shame closing in   he kicks the chair away.

A short drop or regret.

Lights spark.

The cat on a shelf across the garage blurs, drops to the concrete, purrs, and rubs against the tip of his toe. It is soft, warm, a tiny comfort. It will not run for help, will not gnaw at the ties, will not speed the suffocation, will not stop the silent, slow film.

They will be sorry, he thinks or hopes. Or does not.

When they find him, he imagines cheers.   Maybe he knows better
                                                          or not

He wonders if the cat is still there singing in the silence.

He is regret, is sorrow, is sorry or not, is hope and relief, is euphoria and pain, is speeding through thick time, is trapped in freedom.

You and Die

You may have thought about it, may have wondered how it would feel, how best to do it, what people would say or think.

                      Or maybe you didn't care about words and thoughts.

You might have wanted to have the strength to hold the blade to your chest and, without feeling too much pain, slice from throat to pelvic bone and pull out pieces, give a heart to one who refused to go to taco night or to watch reality TV with you, a liver to one who said your writing or habit was too confusing or lacked verisimilitude, a spleen to a superior who refused to promote you despite your having given (actually given) your all to the company or college.

You wanted to pull the intestines out inch by inch to prove a point, to hurt those who hurt you, to show them how they made you feel. You would hand those long, slippery snakes out inch by inch with your unflared nose pointing directly at each recipient, every face muscle relaxed, no scrunch to your chin, your eyes dry and serious. When the gutting was finished and the pieces gifted, you might have wanted to drop gracefully into a mass of beautiful indifference. You might have wanted to return the hurt you'd been issued, wanted peace or revenge, wanted the type of understanding that could only be felt through terror or empathy or comparison.

                      Or maybe you wanted to give thanks by giving yourself away.

You might have wanted to but couldn't.

You might have known the physical pain would outweigh that thing inside that you could not control, knew the blade was insufficient, knew you were too weak to perform, too afraid to push the blade through the skin. You might have hated yourself for being a coward. Or maybe you wanted to feel the ache, knew it would make things better, knew the power of one pain to heal another, knew that, if you could follow through, if you could stay conscious long enough to hand out your little gifts, you would feel euphoria or relief or the warmth of a white-sand beach. You might have started with the blade and began to salivate as droplets of blood ran down your body. This might have made you hate yourself a little bit and more.

                  and made you

Maybe you considered the reality, how the heart was enclosed in a cage to which you had no key, how bends in the river of blood or blinding sorrow or your lack of knowledge of human anatomy would make it difficult to find the gifts you wanted to present. You knew that your studying of organ placement would be lost in a fog once that striking, shiny blade separated your skin into a screaming mouth.

Maybe you never had such feelings, because such feelings belong to the unstable, to the weak or mentally disturbed, to those who should feel shame, to those who are just imagining things, to the attention seekers, to those who chose not to be

                  to those who
chose not to be

                  to those who
chose to be
            normal

Maybe you did not (openly) feel shame. Or you understood shame, attracted it, embodied it, were given little pieces of it every time you called a parent, every time you presented a product of your labors, every time you drove your car or rode your bike, every time you went to the doctor or therapist or your beautician or barber, every time you walked into a gym full of perfection, every time you looked into your crooked mirror.

To show such weakness, you might say, is unacceptable, the only benefit being the farce of normality.

                being normal is like

Maybe you have been thinking about it since you were a child. Maybe you held your breath only to find yourself saved by a spiteful gasp. Maybe you found a rope in the garage and snuck it to your room where you trained yourself in the art of the noose crafted from memories of those used in old Westerns for hangings where the bad or black or falsely accused quickly dropped into a pendulum. Maybe you walked the park or woods or your back yard hunting for a high, strong branch over a pleasant place to die. Maybe you had the perfect horse in mind. Of course, you failed to carry out your plan, returned to your work, to your home, to your bedroom where you learned to smile with your face, even when you wanted to

                                        even when you wanted
                                        something else

Maybe your weirdness had you wearing your best outfit on a freshly bathed body before you would stretch out on the kitchen floor to die. You didn't want to be any trouble. They wouldn't have to clean you up or carry you down the stairs or decide what to bury you in, you had saved them this work. After all, it was you and your dirty room or your inability to score on that test or failure do your chores quick enough or your stupid, greedy ways who caused the screaming, the dish throwing, the dog kicking, the divorce, the riffle shots. This, you thought, would give you a tiny voice, would allow you to really stop breathing and die. This would make things better for everybody. This was to be your gift. A gift you could not give at the time.

                    f a i l u r e
                            failure
                                            F

Maybe the only way you could fall asleep at night was to pretend you were dead. Maybe those dreamy moments were what kept you alive. You would straighten your body, rest your thick head deep into the feather pillow that once belonged to your dead grandmother, pillow holding the memories of the only person who ever *really* loved you, cradling your thoughts, inviting you to return to her arms, giving you a moment of

Giving you a moment of her inviting you to her world of fried chicken and lilacs and orange perfume, inviting you to her world of peace and death.

The sleep lasting only minutes before ideas began to boil deep inside, your stomach somersaulting, your insides expanding, the heat causing organs to itch, each vein trying to work its way through your skin, your bones twitching, marrow bubbling, your skin beginning to stretch until you thought it would give way and the whole mess burst onto your ceiling. The sleep lasting only minutes before shame snuck into your budding dream forcing it to nightmare. The sleep lasting only minutes before your realized that you might have forgot to turn off the coffee pot or iron or that you left the toaster plugged in and, like you were warned, would catch your kitchen on fire and kill everyone in your building including the old woman who reminded you of spring and the little boy downstairs who smelled like cotton candy. The sleep lasting only minutes before your need to run the sweeper or read that book you bought three years ago or polish the leaves of your house plants kicked you into motion. Thoughts break apart the happy scene unraveling in your dream world.

Understanding how it felt to feel broken, without knowing what you were doing, because you never really knew what you were doing, because your insufficiency was spectacular, because you felt comfort in the pleasure of others, you began think of ways to make others happy. Maybe you gave of yourself as a study partner or editor or child laborer or young lover in order to make others smile. Maybe you gave your happiness. Maybe you told jokes about your deepest insecurities (your smile, your height, your lack of intellect, your uneven gait, your pocked face, your inability to keep up at work, you failure to have scrubbed your floors this week or year, your failure to finish school or your book or doing your dishes, your unwillingness to meet new people, your stuttering, your mental stuttering, you incapacity to think on the spot or to just think, your lack of wit, your use of bad similes). Maybe you could never grow a tomato plant or baby in the way you could grow shame.

Maybe you gave

                and gave

You gave

      but really, you were too selfish to give, could only think of yourself, could only do those disguisting things that made people ~~dislike~~ ~~deplore~~ ~~despise~~ Hate ~~you~~

They expected things you ~~could~~ would not give.

                              things like

Your insides turned like

You were as bad as

Your mind was as chaotic as

Your soul as empty as

Your eyes dark as

Not your eyes but your

Your sleep as fleeting as

All of this adds up to

You were never good at math, at words, at speaking, at school, at work, at words, at

You never had the guts to metaphor when you failed at making simile.

You did one brilliant thing. You wrote this amazing line or made the perfect baby or drove for twenty years without getting a ticket. You could paint a wall like a blue-collar Picasso or wait on others like a movie-star butler or saved the life of a cat or fly or dog. You told one good joke, had one nice comeback. You were a smartass

      or a dumbass.

An ass. You were an ass.

You did one brilliant thing that wasn't so brilliant. You did one marginally brilliant thing that grew expectations. You did one marginally brilliant thing that grew expectations you could not live up to. You did one thing

    There were expectations   you could

                                                       not

                                                       live

Maybe you practiced jokes in front of the mirror. You never cracked but imagined others laughing loud and hard, imagined what it might feel like to laugh with them, how a single moment could temper a hundred others. Maybe you imagined conversations, practiced clever comebacks, practiced timing and speed. You watched Carson and tried to outmaneuver McMahon, tried to predict or improve Johnny's lines.

You were a mass of rehearsed SNL sketches waiting for

You were waiting

You were like

You were as

Things you waited for never came.

Things you were you never really were.

You were that which you hated most.

You were a

You were a cliché, a failed metaphor.

You were no Eddie Murphy, no Gilda Radner, no Steve Martin.

You could not satisfy.

                Not yourself.

                               Not

You (never really) gave but wanted to give the pleasure of those slippery, red gifts.

          The best gift of all, you thought

You wanted to give the gift of not being but you didn't.
You couldn't.

Not at that particular moment.

"Uncaged" and "You and Die" were originally published in *Unlikely Stories Mark V* (2016).

from "Exit Interview"
Amy L. Eggert

Mama, They Cry

        Baby   feverish screaming thing
   sick   not its, her fault   nights without
    older child insecure clinging needing
Mama, they cry   craving his, husband's presence
   assistance   gone   alone with both   lonely
  days without   both fluish angry needing   not
their fault   hungry   homework   nights without
   can't sleep, doesn't   doctor says just one pill
      per   small hands stretching, reaching
  must watch them closely   always   loads of
   laundry hungry exhaustion   just one pill
   bedwetting wakes older   regression   consoling
   clean sheets   back to bed   can't sleep, doesn't
   days without   teething tempers tantrums   for
 days   exhaustion   small hands stretching, reaching
     a slap   tears   nights without   just one
pill   not their fault   waking to quiet cries bad
   dreams hungry missing daddy   Mama, they
  whine   phone a scrape tears stitches   should
   have been watching closer   consoling   should
have been   just one pill   one more   missed school bus
      to get in time speeding   pulled over
   baby   purple screaming thing   days without
   signing his, husband's papers   one more pill
  burnt breakfast   both complaining needing hungry
   not their fault   just one more   mounds of
   dirty laundry dirty dishes dirty diapers   always
    one more pill   bickering   just one more
world blurs   older has outgrown clothes needing

           one more   world blurs   baby closes
     fingers in cabinet stretching, reaching needing
      should have been   one more   watching   one
 more   Mama   one more   they cry   world blurs
         quiets slips sinking passing away
        hours without   won't wake, doesn't
         Mama, they cry and cry   sleep.

Ravenous

When news breaks about the dead boy, his classmates respond first
with "Who's he?" and "How'd he die?" and "Wait, who?"

The nobody, his nameless face slipped from minds, fallen between
cracks, drawn blank, illuminated now with sudden starved interest.

The spotlight shifts. And soon, he is everyone's best friend.

A belt in his closet or a gun his mom kept for protection or a bottle
of drain cleaner or a stockpile of pills, it doesn't matter

that none of these are true; gossip mounts. Words have ways
of inflating, of distending to fill gaps and tedium, those delicious

melancholic details neglected by obituaries and morning
announcements and grave moments of tittering silence.

His peers pry, squeeze, poke, shove into his deathstory.
They clasp and claw at his coffin, longing for one last look or,

rather, a long look at the last of him. They parade their heartache,
but it's okay

because they are, after all, the best of friends.

Grief counselors swarm as suicide spreads, a savage appetite swelling,
like a rumor, a contagion, like homo and like fagot and like retard,

like notes scrawled anonymous, slipped through slots in lockers, like
you'd be better off and you should just and why don't you do us all

a favor, like text messages scrolled through by a mom on her knees, like high school hallways decked out in yearbook photos, the charismatic

smile of a happy boy, like strewn poster boards with *RIP* and *we'll miss you*, name misspelled on some, like tears in gym class, *I just can't

today*. He is their best friend.

Sensory overload: Over his corpse, they moan, mourn. Yet inside their crying mouths, the knuckles of their tongues still tingle with the faint taste of bruised flesh.

They consume him.

"Mama, They Cry" was originally published in *Unlikely Stories Mark V* (2016) and "Ravenous" was originally published in *Bluffs Literary Magazine III* (2016).

Author Biographies

Corrie Baldauf knows that humor is the best form of intelligence. She believes that admitting what you don't know is the best way to learn more. She actively seeks opportunities to spend time with people who are not afraid to ask questions. Her art practice is based out of a shared studio space in Corktown, Detroit. She prefers, however, to walk her art around the city of Detroit. Sitting in her studio, she does not think her art seems as alive as it does when it is in the hands of other people. Her Optimism Filter Project was featured in Lille, France at Renaissance. Baldauf's art has appeared in *German Art Magazine*, *Fukt Magazine for Contemporary Drawing*, *Lufthansa Exclusive Magazine*, and *Hyperallergic*. Baldauf is an Assistant Professor of Art at Eastern Michigan University. The main reason she is an instructor is because she thinks there needs to be more scheduled conversations and fewer lectures amongst contemporaries in art. Twitter: @corriebaldauf

Barbara Balfour, a Toronto-based artist, is Professor in the Department of Visual Art and Art History, and Graduate Program Director of the MFA/PhD Graduate Program of Visual Arts at York University in Toronto, Canada. She teaches a graduate course on methods in practice-based research and undergraduate print media and theory courses. Her research involves text-based art practices and print's relationship to multiplicity, with ongoing interest in the phenomenon of the unfinished art project. Balfour has exhibited her artwork internationally. Other activities include artist residencies, conference presentations, critical writing, and curatorial projects—including the two-volume publication/group exhibition *À la recherche (in search of practice-based research)*, at Open Studio, Toronto. Balfour's artist's book *The Inkiest Black* was launched at Katzman Contemporary Gallery, Toronto (2014), and the Los Angeles Art Book Fair (2015). barbarabalfour.ca

G. M. Bettendorf is a 2016 graduate of Rhodes College in Memphis, Tennessee. This fall she will begin doctoral study in English at the Graduate Center of the City University of New York. Though she nurtures enduring and equal fondnesses for John Milton and Virginia Woolf, she is primarily interested in issues of language, consciousness, and embodiment in contemporary American fiction.

Jane L. Carman is a former Sutherland Fellow, founder of the David Foster Wallace Conference, and PhD recipient at Illinois State University. She is founder of the reading series Festival of Language and a reading eXperiment, as well as Lit Fest Press. Her book, *Tangled in Motion*, was published by Journal of Experimental Fiction Books in 2015. Carman's creative and critical work has been anthologized and can be found in *elimae*, *580-Split*, *American Book Review*, *Devil's Lake*, *Palooka*, *Blue Collar Review*, *JAC*, *Santa Clara Review*, among others. festivalwriter@gmail.com

Amy L. Eggert is the author of *Scattershot* (Lit Fest Press 2015), a hybrid collection that redefines and re-envisions the trauma narrative. Additional recent publications can be found in *Unlikely Stories*, *Bluffs Literary Magazine*, and *Festival Writer*. Eggert has a PhD in English Studies from Illinois State University with a specialization in trauma theory and creative writing, and she teaches for Bradley University.

Rhett Farinholt is a PhD candidate in literature at the University of California, San Diego. He received his BA in American literature and culture from UCLA and his MA in literature from California State University, Sacramento. His interests in twentieth and twenty-first century English language literature, disability studies, and psychopharmacology provide the conceptual framework for his ongoing dissertation, "Consider the Pill: Mental Disability and Psychopharmacology in Western Literature after 1952." This work analyzes the shift in literary discourses provoked by—and in response to—the fundamental cultural and clinical move away from psychoanalytic talk therapy toward pharmaceutical prescription in the latter half of the twentieth century. Rhett has presented his research at conferences on a number of topics from the post WWII period, including the works of David Foster Wallace and Will Self.

Professor **Melissa Holton** has taught literature and composition at Austin Community College for more than 20 years. She created a course titled "Gothic Literature and Its Popular Accomplices" for the honors program at Austin Community College in 2010 and teaches the course every year. Looking at the Gothic in literature is both her delight and her job. She lives in Austin, Texas with her math professor husband, Lee Kyle, and their two dogs, Betty and Evie.

Jeff Jarot is a writer who teaches high school English. He holds a BA in English from Illinois Wesleyan University, a BA in English Education and MA in English from Illinois State University, and an MA in English from Northern Illinois University. His short story "Home Movies" appeared in *Festival Writer*. In addition, Jarot's previous Wallace scholarship was featured in *Normal 2014: Selected Works from The First Annual DFW Conference*, as well as *Normal 2015: Selected Works from The Second Annual DFW Conference*. His novella *Zuzu's Petals* was published in February 2016 by Lit Fest Press. Jarot lives in Plainfield, Illinois with his wife and three children and is currently at work on his second novel.

Carissa Kampmeier earned a Master's degree in English Studies from Illinois State University. Her research interests include the ways that contemporary American fiction is both reacting to and influenced by the postmodern movement, the genre of the mixtape as a form of life-writing, and the critical analysis of horror films.

Ashlie M. Kontos is a master's student of English at the University of Texas at Tyler. Her research interests include shame; literary theory—specifically metamodernism; post-Holocaust Jewish literature; and the literature and philosophy of David Foster Wallace. She has her BA in English with minors in history and classical studies. Her essay "Nomina Nuda Tenemus: Jonathan Safran Foer Finding Meaning Within Empty Names, or (re)Construction of Deconstruction" won the University of Louisiana at Lafayette's Darrell Borque Award (2012) and was published in *Media, Technology, and Imagination* in 2013 by Cambridge Scholars Publishing. Her essay "'It takes great personal courage to let yourself appear weak': DFW on Shame, Addiction and Healing" appeared in *Normal 2014*, which she co-edited in 2015.

Daniel Leonard is a poet and teacher from Pennsylvania. He holds an MFA in creative writing from Boston University, where he received the Hurley Prize and was a 2015 Robert Pinsky Global Fellow. He also holds an MA in philosophy from the University of Leuven and an interdisciplinary degree from Wheaton College. Daniel has written chapters for three volumes of Open Court's *Pop Culture and Philosophy* series. He is the creator of *3eanuts*, a humor website reviewed online by *Time*, *Entertainment Weekly*, and others. He has presented at the DFW Conference each year since its inception, and he supposes he'll do it again.

Ben Leubner lives and teaches in Bozeman, Montana, where he specializes in poetry and poetics. His writing has appeared in *Twentieth-Century Literature*, the *Southwest Review*, *Religion and the Arts*, *3:AM* magazine, *Critical Studies in Improvisation*, and elsewhere.

Brian Monday received his master's degree from Illinois State University, where he earned a Sutherland Fellowship, served as Production Director for the Unit of Contemporary Literature, and studied under Curtis White and David Foster Wallace. He has since taught English at Westosha Central High School in Salem, Wisconsin and has written a book of poems (*A Little Breath*), short stories (*The Klein-Bottle Boy and His Ontological Dilemma*), and, most recently, education-related limericks (*A Locker of Limericks & A Handful of Shorts*). Monday is currently studying the workshop critiques that Wallace offered him and hopes to collect other such critiques in a book that explores the nature of Wallace's teaching. He lives in Trevor, Wisconsin with his wife and two sons. mondaywrites@gmail.com

Melissa Newfield has been pursuing David Foster Wallace studies since 2008. Currently, she teaches Composition at New Mexico Highlands University. She received a master's degree in English Literature in 2009 from NMHU, completing her thesis, "Postmodernization of Redemption: from *Paradise Lost* to *Pulp Fiction*." She writes and lives in Santa Fe, NM and would like to write a book on intertextuality and *Infinite Jest*.

Alexander C. Ruhsenberger was a GTA instructor and MA graduate from Montana State University. Ruhsenberger wrote his thesis on postmodernism and *Infinite Jest*. Ruhsenberger plans on attending a doctoral program working on a project that focuses on what comes after postmodernism. The project will examine various authors, philosophers, and thinkers, who speculate on where digital culture might lead. In the meantime, Ruhsenberger resides in Vancouver, Washington. He plans to write nonfiction on current cultural topics and one day publish his novel about experiences in academia, youth, and romance.

Danny Sheaf holds an Honours degree in English & Creative Arts and philosophy awarded by Murdoch University (Perth, Australia). He completed his honours dissertation in 2014. He is currently a PhD candidate at Murdoch University. Sheaf's research concerns a philosophical engagement with the fiction of David Foster Wallace. He is particularly interested in the phenomenology of Martin Heidegger and Jan Patočka as a way of engaging with contemporary issues.

Tom Winchester holds an MFA in art criticism and writing from School of Visual Arts and has been published in the *Miami Rail*, *OMNI Reboot*, *Hyperallergic*, and *M/E/A/N/I/N/G*. He currently lives and works in Sarasota, Florida.

Books by Lit Fest Press

Beyond Bulrush
by Jeannie E. Roberts

Blasphemer
by Bill Yarrow

Is
by Martin Nakell

Filthy
by Jake Giszczynski and Dominique Jackson

A Grand Sociology Lesson
by KJ Hannah Greenberg

Infinite LEGO: Reimagining David Foster Wallace's
Infinite Jest *Through LEGO*
by Ryan M. Blanck

LIFE+70[REDACTED]
by David Moscovich

Night Chorus
by Joani Reese

Normal 2014: Collected Works from
the First Annual DFW Conference
edited by Emily Brutton, Carissa Kampmeier,
and Ashlie M. Kontos

Normal 2015: Collected Works from
the Second Annual DFW Conference
edited by Carissa Kampmeier, Ashlie M. Kontos,
Brian Monday, and Emily Brutton

Normal 2016: Collected Works from
the ThirdAnnual DFW Conference
edited by Jeff Jarot, Ashlie M. Kontos,
Brian Monday, and Carissa Kampmeier

Pestiferous Questions
by Margaret Rozga

*Proofread or Die!: Collected Works by
Former Students & Colleagues of David Foster Wallace*
edited by Charles B. Harris

Redshift
by Bernd Sauermann

Reliquary of Debt
by Wendy Vardaman

Scattershot: Collected Fictions
by Amy L. Eggert

Scribblings of a Madman
by Paul Tristram

Shibolleth
by James D. Sullivan

Sipping Coffee @ Carmela's
by Joe Amato

Standards of Sadiddy
by Jonathan Penton

We are traveling through dark at trememdous speeds.
by Sarah Sadie

The Whisper Gallery
by Nate Maxson

Zuzu's Petals
by Jeff Jarot

Forthcoming from Lit Fest Press

Blue Unicorn: Stories
by Stephen Spotte

The Chronicles of Michel du Jabot
by Eckhard Gerdes

Circe's Bicycle
by Tara Campbell

How I Pitched the First Curve
by Ryan Clark

It Was Me
by Nicholas A. Klein

Literary Yoga: Exercises for Those Who Can Write
by Yuriy Tarnawsky

The Moment of Capture
by John Lambremont Sr.

Rush's Deal
by A.S. Coomer

To Deer at Swim
by Jamison Lee

We're Going to Need a Higher Fence
(2016 Lit Fest Press Book Contest Winner)
by Jennifer MacBain-Stephens

What to Do with Red
(2016 Lit Fest Press Book Contest Winner)
by Jacquelyn "Jacsun" Shah

www.ingramcontent.com/pod-product-compliance
Lightning Source LLC
Chambersburg PA
CBHW070555160426
43199CB00014B/2517